ART, THE CRITICS, AND YOU

ART THE CRITICS AND YOU

By CURT J. DUCASSE

Professor of Philosophy, Brown University

NEW YORK
OSKAR PIEST
1944

PREFACE

THE ARTIST and the philosopher are two men regarded by the general public with a certain bewilderment, compounded of respect and mistrust, mild scorn and envy, impatience and wonder. The philosopher is popularly conceived as an impractical being, so deeply plunged in abstract thought that he does not even see where he walks and cannot recognize his wife when he meets her at the train unless he takes along her photograph. His words, moreover, are often irritatingly obscure; and this has moved one of philosophy's own devotees to describe it facetiously as "the systematic abuse of an elaborate technical terminology invented especially for the purpose." Yet so important have the writings of some philosophers been considered that study of them has persisted through century after century; and some philosophical ideas have been recognized as potentially so dynamic that more than one philosopher has had to pay for expressing them with his liberty or even his life.

The artist is commonly thought of as perhaps less dangerous but no less queer. He is pictured as a long-haired creature who wears odd clothes, whose habitat is a garret, and who lives an ill-regulated,

bohemian existence. More impractical still than the
philosopher, he barely manages to avoid starvation.
Yet he sometimes creates things of arresting beauty;
and were it not that at other times he produces with
the same fervor incomprehensible or perversely
bizarre works, one would be tempted to believe that
his madness is indeed of the kind which, in Plato's
Phaedrus, Socrates describes as inspired by the
Muses.

In these pages, one of these two odd creatures is
going to talk about the other. The philosopher, in
his more specific role of aesthetician or philosopher
of art, is going to discuss the artist, his public, and
his critics; and will try to answer a number of questions about them that thrust themselves forward as
soon as attention is turned on the respective activities of these three classes of men.

In the very act of discussing these questions, however, the aesthetician will be exhibiting concretely
the nature of the enterprise of aesthetics, in which
he himself is engaged. The task of the first chapter
will be to describe this enterprise; to show how it is
related on the one hand to art and on the other to
philosophy in general; and to make evident that the
problems of aesthetics are not remote and only academic, but on the contrary are likely to have at times
passionately engaged most of us.

The next four chapters will outline the essentials
of a philosophy of art presented by the author in
an earlier book entitled, *The Philosophy of Art,*
which has now been out of print for a number of

years. These chapters are an expansion of the contents of three public lectures delivered by him at the University of Illinois, in the spring of 1942.

In the sixth chapter, attention will be called to the importance of education of the feelings as an integral part of the education of a human being; and to the fact that, in education of the feelings, the works of the various free and decorative arts have a role to play analogous to that of scientific treatises in education of the mind for activity in the fields of science.

The seventh chapter will attempt to anatomize and to shield from undue contempt the one among the decorative arts that alone is practised by almost everyone, namely, the cosmetic art.

The earlier, more detailed, and more technical book mentioned above was intended primarily for aestheticians and formal students of the philosophy of art. The present volume, on the other hand, is addressed rather to the many more persons who, in the course of ordinary life, enjoy music or paintings, poems or other literary works, the drama, the ballet, or other forms of art; and who, in addition, have a general reader's normal degree of curiosity concerning their own interest in objects of these kinds and in what they hear said about them.

Such "consumers" of art often are awed and bewildered by the comments or judgments made upon works of the various arts by the persons who pass as connoisseurs of them. The technical language the latter employ wraps the arts in a mantle of mystery, and fosters the false belief that painters and poets paint and write for other painters and poets, or for a species of initiates called critics, but not for ordinary men. These, accordingly, are likely to feel that it is somewhat presumptuous on their part to venture to like or dislike, in their own honest but unlearned way, the works that artists of the various arts nevertheless display before them and hope they will buy.

It is to these persons, who too easily allow themselves to feel slightly ashamed of being "only" amateurs of the arts, that this book is dedicated. It seeks to provide them with the text of a declaration of independence in matters of taste in art; and to encourage them to cultivate their own taste through abundant and varied but always positive exercise thereof, rather than passively by allowing it to be molded into the shape of the taste of some supposed authority. The latter device merely puts one's taste in a spiritual corset, the wearing of which confers an appearance of culture that not only fools none but fools, but is paid for in the end by atrophy of the muscles of one's own taste.

Chapters VI and VII have appeared in slightly different form as articles in *The American Scholar*, under the titles of, respectively, *Are the Humanities Worth Their Keep?* and *The Animal with Red Cheeks*. Thanks are due the editor of this journal for his kind permission to make use of the contents of these two articles here.

C. J. DUCASSE

Providence, Rhode Island
June 7, 1944.

CONTENTS

ART, THE CRITICS, AND YOU

ARTIST, AMATEUR, AND CRITIC

B Y WAY OF MAKING A START on the task of this chapter, I shall ask the reader to translate himself in thought to the depths of a certain cave in the south of France, in the remote past of twenty thousand years ago. By the light of a stone lamp or of a torch of resinous wood, one of the ancestors of the men of today was at work there, engraving and painting upon the walls of the cave pictures of mammoth, bison, and other animals now extinct or no longer found in that part of the world.

One might expect a man who lived in prehistoric times to have been a primitive savage, possessed of but rude skills, and these only of the most directly practical sorts. Yet some of these ancient cave pictures, instead of being naïve and crude, exhibit a mastery of line equal to that of the best draughtsmen of today. And so keenly observant were the men of that remote epoch that they had perceived some things rediscovered by modern man but a few decades ago, and then only with the aid of instantaneous photographs. For example, the position of the legs of a galloping animal, which until recently was incorrectly represented in most of our paintings, is correctly depicted on a piece of engraved bone unearthed in another French cave.

Art, or at least graphic art, is proved by these cave drawings to be a very ancient human activity; but it is also one well-nigh universal. From the tropic to the arctic regions, there is hardly a tribe known, however primitive, that does not have some form of art. It is true that the patterns drawn, the dramas enacted, the chants and the dances performed, are generally believed by participants and spectators alike to have religious or magical effects, and that this is a motive or the chief motive for these activities. They are thus not instances of art for art's sake; but this does not mean that they are any the less genuinely art. Throughout history, the art impulse has depended for its opportunities in large part upon practical, religious, or other needs, which required that some useful object be created or some supposedly efficacious ceremony performed. But the patterns or other forms prescribed for these by their practical or other ends are hardly ever so closely specified as not to leave considerable room for the expression of the maker's or performer's own taste in their execution. Need arises, for instance, to make a spoon; and the use to which it is to be put prescribes, in a general way, the size and shape of the bowl and the handle. But within the limits thus set by the function to be performed, much freedom remains for expression of the maker's individual taste in shaping handle and bowl. To

this extent, the spoon he creates is not merely a
work of practical art but, in addition, genuinely a
work of aesthetic art.

Objects created primarily for the sake of their
practical utility are thus not only an opportunity
for the artistic imagination of the maker, but also
an opportunity for aesthetic enjoyment on the part
of the user. Man is seldom content to have the instruments of his daily activities—his houses, furniture, clothing, typewriters, automobiles, and so on
—satisfy only the practical needs for the sake of
which they were made. He demands, in addition,
that their shapes, materials, and other perceptible
features shall be pleasing to his senses. And so insistent is this demand that we have to look a long
time among the countless objects of everyday use to
find one where the attempt to give it aesthetic appeal has not been made; and where much thought,
labor, and money has not been expended for this,
beyond what would have sufficed for the object's
purely practical functions.

There is thus evidence on every side that art and
aesthetic interest are phenomena as truly intrinsic
to human life and as distinctive of it as are, for instance, religion, science, or trade. Yet—paradoxic-
ally, in these days of universal familiarity with the
notion that any trait that survives must have had
some value for the survival of its possessor—art and
its products have no very obvious biological or social
utility. They have the appearance of being luxuries,

which it is pleasant indeed to have but without which man could be just as healthy, vigorous, and successful in the control of his environment.

The question thus forces itself upon us whether there are not, after all, some hidden but important functions that art discharges and that account for its having survived through the ages, notwithstanding its great cost. Or, we may wonder whether the truth is not perhaps rather that man is fundamentally not, as is so lightly assumed, a practical being, but a playboy, a dreamer, or an apprentice god, who indeed heeds practical considerations so far as he must but whose superior intelligence and efficiency leave him time and energy for pursuits and experiences that, although they have no instrumental worth, have the self-justifying immediate worth of being enjoyed by him and constitute the meaning that distinguishes human from merely animal life.

Obviously, this question regarding the role and proper place of art and its products in the life of man cannot be answered with any confidence until another has been cleared up, namely: What exactly is this thing that we call art?

It is true that some persons suppose that a statement of the functions of art in human life would constitute an answer to the question as to what art is; but this is as great a mistake as the belief, also held by some, that the question as to the nature of a given thing is answered by saying how it came to be as it is. The purposes to which a thing may be put are but corollaries of the nature of the thing;

and an account of the evolutionary or other process by which it came to have the nature it does have is not an account of what, specifically, this nature is. To inquire into the nature of art is to ask, for instance, whether "art" is perhaps the name of some perceptible quality that pervades alike paintings, musical compositions, sculptures, poems, cathedrals, and other objects called works of art; or whether, possibly, "art" is not rather the name of some form of human activity, and if so what exactly is its description. Is it a special form of play? Or is it nothing more than a subtle means the artist employs to attract a desired mate? Or is it a special form of language? Or again, is it only a spontaneous expression of emotional exuberance? Or is it perhaps simply the manifestation of a human craving to behold beautiful things?

But before we can gauge objectively the role of art in the life of mankind, there is another question to be answered, as important as that of the nature of art and closely connected with it. For a work of art is not merely something that somebody creates, but is also something that other persons can and do contemplate. There is to art, in most instances, a receiving end as well as a producing end. Beside the artists who create poems, dramas, paintings, statues, ballets, and symphonies, there are also the far more numerous persons who read books, attend dramatic performances, look at paintings, and listen to music. These I like to call the *consumers* of art, to distinguish them from the persons who are called critics and whose pronouncements concerning the merits of the works they discuss are supposed to be in some sense and to some extent authoritative. The consumers of art, on the other hand, do not regard themselves as authorities; but tend rather to be humble, if not apologetic, about their tastes. They are the ordinary amateurs of music, literature, pictures, or the theater.

It is true that the terms "amateur" and "dilettante" alike are often used with a certain derogatory connotation. They have acquired it, of course, in contexts where some objective achievement was being attempted that required professional rather than amateur technique. But, strictly speaking, to be an amateur of music, painting, or literature simply means to like such things; and to be a dilettante is to take delight in them. Surely this is nothing blameworthy, but is on the contrary the very sort of interest that insures for art a public. Indeed it is, I believe, to consumers of art in this sense that artists primarily address their works. Shakespeare wrote his plays for the ordinary amateurs of the theater of his day, not for dissecting professors of literature; and Beethoven composed his music for ordinary concertgoers, not for musicologists—who, it may be recalled, have been facetiously described by someone as people who "know all about music but hate the sound of it"!

Thus, beside the sort of interest that moves some men to the creation of works of art, there is also the sort of interest that moves many more to the contemplation of them. And our second question concerns the nature of this contemplation. The question is, more particularly: What sort of an attitude is aesthetic contemplation? How is it related to simple attention? How does it differ from curiosity and from pragmatic interest? What sorts of conditions are favorable or unfavorable to it? What kinds of effects does it have on those who engage in it? What sort of preparation, if any, does it require in them? And what modes of appreciation of works of art, other than aesthetic appreciation, may be possible or legitimate?

But beside the two sorts of interest that animate respectively the creator and the consumer of works of art, there is yet a third sort to which I have so far only alluded in passing, namely, the critical interest —the interest of the person who analyzes and discusses particular works of art, and who passes judgments concerning their relative merits. The questions that arise in connection with the criticism of works of art are, for example: What is or can be meant by speaking of a given work of art as good or bad, or as better or worse than another? Who, if anybody, is qualified to pass judgment as to its merit? Of what nature are the standards used in making this judgment, and in what sense may these standards themselves be said to be valid or invalid? It is questions such as these that are comprised in the general problem of the nature of literary criticism and of the criticism of works of the other arts.

The Aesthetician's Task

The remarks that have been made up to this point
have brought out that, in connection with concrete
works of art, there are, then, three typical kinds of
human activity that may be and in many cases are engaged in by one and the same person, but that are
nevertheless distinguishable and susceptible of occur-
ring to some extent independently. These three types
of activity are the creation of works of art, aesthetic
contemplation of them, and criticism of them; and
no enlightened view of the role of art and of its products in the life of man is possible so long as our conception of these three activities remains as vague as
ordinarily it is.

I shall not at this point attempt to analyze these
activities, but shall leave that to the following chapters. Rather, I wish now especially to call attention to
the fact that, in what has preceded, we too have been
occupying ourselves with art; and yet we have not
been doing at all what is done by the artist or by the
consumer of art or by the art critic. That is, we have
neither been creating works of art, nor contemplating or criticizing any. We have been doing something
quite different; we have been attending to the kinds
of activity in which the artist, the consumer, and the
critic, respectively, are engaged; and we have been
asking certain questions about the nature of these
activities.

The impulse that has motivated us has thus been
neither the creative nor the contemplative nor the

evaluative, but the inquisitive. This impulse—curiosity, or the craving for knowledge—is the one that animates also the scientist, whom we therefore in so far resemble. But we differ from him in that the knowledge we seek concerns not any of the realms of nature that man confronts, but instead certain of the purposive activities of man himself as he confronts nature and his fellow men.

And now the question arises: To whom are we to turn for answers to the questions we have asked about the three typical sorts of activity we have noticed? Who is the man that has made it his specific task to inquire into these matters systematically and who, therefore, instead of only hasty opinions concerning them, may be expected to have something approximating true knowledge of them?

It is a popular notion that, for knowledge concerning any given mode of human activity, one should go to those persons who are expert in the performance of it—here, for instance, to the artist. But this notion, although plausible at first sight, is nevertheless mostly mistaken. Matisse, himself a great artist, has pointed out that the painter expresses himself in paint, and that what he says is not important. As Oscar Wilde remarked long ago, doing is one thing and discoursing is another. Expertness in one does not automatically entail expertness in the other.

Digesting our food, for example, is a very complex feat of physiological chemistry that most of us perform quite ably but the nature of which, in most instances, we should be very much at a loss to explain.

We know how to do it, but we do not know how we do it. On the other hand, a physiologist could tell us a great deal about it, even if he himself happened to be a dyspeptic hardly able to digest anything. Or, as an example of activity that is voluntary rather than reflex, like digestion, I might mention the one cited by Oscar Wilde himself when he declares that any-body can make history, but only a great man can write it.

It may or may not be true, as Wilde claims, that it is more difficult to talk about a thing than to do it, but at all events one is very different from the other. The gifts, training, and opportunities needed for ob-serving, analyzing, and describing the creative or the contemplative or the critical activity are, for the most part, different from those needed for the perform-ance itself of these activities; and it is only exception-ally that the expert practitioner is also an expert observer, analyst, and describer.

To scrutinize and describe the nature of these ac-tivities is the specific task of the branch of human inquiry called aesthetics, or the philosophy of art. It is true that the aesthetician is seldom himself much of an artist or of an art critic, and may not even be an especially avid consumer of art; but, fortunately, there is no necessity that he should be so. The essen-tial nature of the art-creative activity is the same and can be discerned equally well at the humbler levels on which almost all of us at times engage in one or another of its many forms. The contemplative activ-ity, similarly, can on innumerable everyday occasions be observed in oneself directly, and in others indirectly through their reports. And the critic, whose very business it is to discuss in public the merits of works of art publicly displayed, provides the aesthetician with abundant opportunities to observe what exactly it is that a critic does. But no matter how much or little of an artist, or of an amateur of art, or of an art critic the aesthetician may himself happen to be, his position with regard to the respective forms of activity is essentially that of a spectator curious about them, whose task is to observe them and reflect upon them, and to describe their respective natures, their mutual relations, and their relations to other aspects of the life of man.

How Aesthetics Is Related to Philosophy

To make clear in what precedes the scope of the branch of inquiry called aesthetics, attention was first called to the kinds of concern with art of, respectively, the artist himself, the public, and the critic. Then a number of questions about each of these were mentioned, without answers to which no objective view can be obtained of the role of art or of aesthetic objects in the life of man. Finally, aesthetics was characterized as the undertaking whose specific business it is to investigate methodically these very questions. But additional light on the nature and functions of aesthetics may now be obtained by approaching the subject no longer, as it were, from below—as we do when we define it in terms of concrete examples of the questions it seeks to answer—but instead from above, by exhibiting it as a particular branch of the intellectual enterprise generically called philosophy.

We thus find ourselves led to ask, first, what philosophy itself is. This is one of the most embarrassing questions that may be put to a philosopher; for, as already pointed out, it is one thing to carry on a given activity—whether it be digesting, dancing, philosophizing, or any other—and quite another thing to reflect upon it and to define its nature. Neither the dancer or other artist, nor the physicist, biologist, or other scientist, as such, is required to reflect upon and to define the nature and value of the task in which he is professionally engaged. His business is only to perform it. Indeed, the moment he begins to reflect upon it, he has already abandoned it for the time and undertaken instead an investigation of the philosophy of his subject.

But in the case of the philosopher, the matter stands otherwise: one of the things that it is his task as a philosopher to analyze and define is the very activity in which he himself is engaged when he is philosophizing. This task is probably one of the most difficult he is called upon to perform, but what I conceive to be its right outcome is nothing mysterious and is susceptible of being stated rather simply.

The question, "What is philosophy?" is perhaps best approached by recalling the ancient endeavor to determine what essentially differentiates man from other animals. One of the earlier answers proposed was that man is the only biped that has no feathers. But then someone brought in a plucked chicken, and thereby disposed of that hypothesis. It has been said, also, that man is the animal that cooks his food; but some men subsist on raw food and yet do not cease to be men. The most familiar answer doubtless is that man is the rational animal; but all that can rationally be claimed is that man is the animal who is rational when there is no temptation for him to be otherwise —which is seldom indeed.

There is another answer, suggested long ago by Epictetus and offered by Nietzsche in a passage of his *Thus Spake Zarathustra.* "Man," he there declares, "is the animal with red cheeks!" By this, Nietzsche means that man is the animal that is ashamed of himself, for man's cheeks are red when he blushes, and it is when he is ashamed that he blushes.

The implications of this thought may be further developed by pointing out that the occasions on which man feels shame are those on which he notices that he is falling short of one or another of his ideals. Man, therefore, is the animal that has ideals as to what he should do and think and feel and be. And this further implies that man is the animal who is capable of observing himself; and who is interested in doing so, and in evaluating and attempting to improve the self that he discovers to be his at the time. Man, we might thus say—and this, of course, includes woman—is the animal that lives before a mirror!

The mirror is at times a literal, physical mirror,

which reflects his or her outward appearance—too often, alas, a horrible sight that sends her, at least, screaming for help to the beauty parlor! Thus the employment of cosmetics unexpectedly turns out to be akin to the more respected practices called prayer and meditation, in that it too is a manifestation of the idealism—the striving after self-improvement— that is one of the deepest and most distinctive human impulses. The philosophy of cosmetics is a fascinating subject, and will be considered by itself in a later chapter. At this point, therefore, I pass it over with only these few words, since what now needs to be emphasized is that the mirror before which man lives is not always a physical mirror but often, and more profoundly, a mental mirror—the mirror which, significantly, we call *reflection* on what we are, do, feel, think, desire, or attempt. It is this mirror that we are using when we meditate on our own lives, and then embody in prayers to our god our longings for nearer approach to the perfection that we discover we lack.

Now the answer I would give to the question, "What is philosophy?" is that *philosophy consists in the sort of reflection by which we seek to make clear to ourselves what exactly we are intending to assert, with regard to the things of all sorts we criticize every day, by the various adjectives of appraisal we apply to them.* For example, just what do we mean to assert about a given opinion when we appraise it as *erroneous* or *sound,* about a given act when we call it *morally right* or *morally wrong,* about a given piece of reasoning when we label it *valid* or *fallacious,* about a given consideration when we term it *important* or *unimportant,* about a given object when we judge it *real* or *illusory,* or about a given effect when we call it *artistic* or *sublime* or *ugly?* Doubt often remains as to the justness of such appraisals of given things if we do not know clearly what it is we are asserting in them about those things.

But when we attempt to make it clear to ourselves, we quickly see that another question is intimately tied up with this—the question as to the class to which a thing must belong in order that a given one of these adjectives of criticism be applicable to it (whether affirmatively or negatively) without incongruity. For example, to scratch oneself when one itches or to choose pumpkin pie rather than squash pie for dessert is not the sort of action about which it would ordinarily be congruous to say either that it is morally right or morally wrong. Just what, then, marks off the things to which alone criticism in moral terms is relevant? This question, too, is a philosophical question, as are those analogous to it in the case of the other adjectives of appraisal.

Are such questions important? The criticisms—whether ethical, logical, aesthetic, or other—that we formulate by adjectives such as exemplified above all have practical importance, because *each of these adjectives is a verbal trigger that, as occasion presents itself, releases actions adapted to suppress or alter, or on the contrary to defend or foster, the thing to which we applied the adjective.* It is of moment to ourselves and to others who may be affected by our actions or moved by our words to act similarly that we should apply those adjectives *justly;* for, let it be well noted, they act as triggers of action irrespective of whether in a given case we were justified or mistaken in applying them. If we were mistaken, then the course of action their application releases is folly and stultifies us. But, as already pointed out, there are many instances where, because we know only vaguely what we mean by such adjectives of criticism, doubts arise as to whether or not we are applying them justly. To know their meaning clearly is then important.

When we become aware that we are facing an instance in which this is important, then we naturally try, by reflection, to gain the clearness we need; and such reflection is philosophical reflection. But, with most of us, reflection of this sort is perforce sporadic only, carried on with little or no method, and confined to problems that thrust themselves on our attention because they are directly connected with our personal concerns and environment. Our reflection on such occasions is none the less truly philosophical but is then not very searching nor very assured, nor of very wide scope. Rather, it is in these respects on a level with the knoweldge of the laws of nature that all men acquire in the course of their dealing with nature merely at the level of common experience. But just as what we call natural science consists of the much firmer, more precise, and more far-reaching knowledge of nature that can be obtained through careful laboratory procedures, so does philosophy,

when scientifically pursued, consist in the method-
ical, painstaking, and persistent sort of investigation
that, in the matters just described as anywhere else,
alone can yield knowledge as distinguished from wish-
ful opinions, prejudices, hasty generalizations, and
the like. The philosopher, like the natural scientist,
thus only tries to get better knowledge of certain
things that every man, at times and after a fashion,
tries to know.

But it is important to realize that—equally in the
field of the natural sciences or in that of philosophy—
knowledge thus genuine is, in part but necessarily,
based on the theory of the subject it concerns. That
is, it results in part from the construction of theories
that demonstrably explain the facts of the given field
—of theories that, although they are indeed theories,
are rigorously subjected to the empirical control,
without which they would remain only empty specu-
lations. But theory, unavoidably, is always more or
less technical; and thus philosophy, like natural
science, has theoretical and technical parts.

Now philosophy, insofar as its theoretical parts are
concerned, might be described as the "general theory
of criticism." But in terms of the humanistic aim
that, for most persons, must be what ultimately vin-
dicates the technicalities to which philosophy sometimes needs to resort, philosophy is more enlighten-
ingly described as "the search for the kind of knowledge specifically called wisdom." And wisdom, let it
be realized, is knowledge of norms—knowledge of
what, in the varieties of circumstances men face, one

ought and ought not to do, feel, think, or strive for if he is to gain from life what he most deeply craves from it. Philosophy, accordingly, may also be distinguished, as normative science, from the natural and the formal sciences. But just as the natural sciences, for instance, do not prescribe laws to nature but merely attempt to discover, describe, and explain nature's laws, so likewise philosophy is not normative in the sense that it prescribes norms of thought, action, or feeling, but only in the sense that it seeks to discover these norms, to describe them and their interrelations, and to explain them.

Aesthetics, or the philosophy of art, is one particular branch of the general enterprise thus characterized—the branch that seeks wisdom concerning, specifically, art, aesthetic contemplation, and the criticism of literature and the other arts. Aesthetics seeks the inclusive perspective on these matters and the accompanying sense of relative values that are the only effective vaccines against the countless catchwords, dogmas, half-baked theories, and personal predilections, erected into would-be authoritative standards, that infest the world of art and criticism and shroud it in the mystery of confusion.

What Occasions Make Us Philosophize about Art

Because this account of the nature of philosophy and of aesthetics as a branch of philosophy was perforce framed in somewhat abstract terms, it will perhaps have caused an impression that philosophizing

—including philosophizing on the subject of art—is something essentially academical and remote from the lives of all but a few of us. Now, therefore, something should be said to make further evident that, on the contrary, philosophizing—and philosophizing on that subject—is something in which most of us at times do engage spontaneously and indeed vigorously, although we do so perhaps unawares—like the man in Molière's play, who, unawares also, had been speaking all his life in prose.

That each of us is likely more than once to have taken at least some steps of his own in the field of the philosophy of art will be made evident if attention is called to the type of situation that irresistibly provokes almost anyone to do so, namely, those occasions on which our own judgment concerning some matter connected with art clashes with the judgment of another person.

The judgment may concern the merits of a given painting, of a given book, or of a work of some other art; or it may perhaps concern the propriety of the use of certain technical means of creation, or the appropriateness of a certain mode of response to a given work. For example, the judgment challenged might be that, in painting, to use an air brush is not "cricket"; or that an etcher who draws from photographs, instead of always directly from nature, is cheating. Or, again, the judgment might be that, for the right appreciation of painting, the subject represented ought to be disregarded; or that what a painter ought essentially to aim at is exhibition of the plastic characters of objects and their relations in space; or perhaps that enjoyment of paintings without analysis of them is fatuous. Or, to mention yet other examples, the assertion challenged might be that art ought to be engaged in only for art's sake and not, let us say, for the sake of propaganda; or that art and its products are a luxury; or that the only right standard in terms of which to evaluate works of art is their bearing on the moral improvement of mankind; and so on. All of us, doubtless, can recall having heard and probably having taken part in discussions where the matter in dispute was some such proposition as those just mentioned.

But let us now notice the course that discussions of this kind inevitably take and the steps in that course which constitute the propounding of at least fragments of a philosophy of art spontaneously constructed to defend the position one has taken. To make the matter as clear as possible, let us take a concrete example. Let us suppose that someone, after examining a certain painting, pronounces it bad, whereas we judge it to be good; and that, when asked why he considers it bad, this person answers that it is because the painting does not bring out vividly the voluminousness—the space-filling character and the relations in deep space—of the objects represented. And let us suppose further that, although we grant the painting indeed makes little of the third dimension of space, we deny that this constitutes a defect. How, in such a case, does the person whose appraisal we have challenged go about vindicating it? Or, equally, how do we go about supporting our own position?

Whenever the dispute does not degenerate into a mere quarrel—in which shouting and the hurling of epithets takes the place of argument—but rather seeks genuinely a rational solution of the conflict, what occurs is this: The person whose judgment we challenge reaches instinctively for some more abstract and general statement of what are the essential aims of painting, to the end of then showing that these aims are served by a vivid representation of the plastic aspects of objects.

Such a major premise—as logicians would call it— by which to support one's condemnation of the given painting, might, for example, be that the essential business of painting is to represent reality as faithfully as possible. This proposition, obviously, constitutes a fragment or the embryo of a philosophy of art, or at least of painting. It will perhaps be said— and, I grant, with truth—that it is not a very plausible theory as to the essential aims of painting, and thus brings but rather weak support to the reason that was given for condemning the painting. But aesthetic theories that are, like this, picked out of the air under the pressure of attack are seldom profound or very defensible. They are advanced because the position one maintains obviously is supported, or seems to be supported, by them; and just because they are so transparently *ad hoc,* they are themselves quickly challenged by the opponent.

What then occurs? Very much the same sort of

thing over again, but this time at a more abstract level. That is, the disputants find themselves driven to seek some still more general major premise—some more abstract proposition as to the essential aims of painting or, perhaps even more abstractly, of art in general—on which they may be able to agree. And, let it be noted, the possibility of such agreement increases with the degree of abstractness of the proposition. For the more abstract the proposition, the less immediately obvious are its bearings on the particular case in dispute; and hence the easier it is for both parties to consider it candidly on its own merits, instead of only on the basis of whether it bears out the original contention of one or of the other.

A high major premise on which they might eventually find themselves able to agree would be, for example, the one on which Tolstoi built his own philosophy of art, namely, that art is the deliberate attempt by one man to transmit to others—by means of lines, colors, sounds, and so forth—feelings he himself has experienced. The two disputants would then next have to inquire what demonstrable implications this conception of art, which we suppose them both to accept, has concerning the merits of the painting before them. In this way they may reach a decision that is rational, in the sense of being logically deducible from a high major premise they both regard as true.

It is of course seldom that, in the discussions we all at times engage in when such matters are in dispute, the movement of argument just illustrated develops in an orderly manner or progresses to a conclusion that resolves the dispute; for usually there is more heat than method in such discussions. Moreover, they are not prolonged beyond perhaps an hour or two; and the questions implicitly involved in the disagreement that originates the dispute are so numerous, and some of them often so difficult, that in that short time only a little progress could be made, even if the inquiry were conducted in as systematic a manner as it should be.

But the foregoing example and analysis will, I hope, have sufficed to show that disputes of this general sort, even when unsystematic, are genuinely disputes about the philosophy of art; and that, since most of us at times do take part in them, the philosophy of art is not something cultivated only in academic halls, but rather something about which we occasionally get so heated that perhaps for a week afterward we will not speak to the friend who opposed us! The difference between most of us and professional aestheticians is thus only that these same questions, which we discuss but informally with a friend, are investigated by the aesthetician more patiently and methodically, and in all their hidden though vital ramifications.

From the attempt in this chapter to indicate the scope and function of aesthetics and to convict the reader of possessing an interest, perhaps not recognized by him as being such, in its problems, I now pass to the most fundamental question, namely: What essentially is this activity called art?

CHAPTER II

ART AS NATURAL TO MAN AS SPEECH

W HAT IS ART? Certainly it is not, as sometimes assumed, a quality ingredient alike in paintings, musical compositions, statues, poems, cathedrals, and so on; for these things are not instances of art but of works—that is, of products—of art. Art itself is much rather a species of human activity.

The word "art," taken in its broadest sense, means skill; and skill is capacity so to control an activity that it, or its products, shall have certain intended characteristics. Thus any kind of activity, insofar as it is skilled, is a species of art. But when mention is made of art or of the arts without qualification, the reference usually is neither to the practical arts—such as medicine, husbandry and shoemaking—nor to the sportive arts—that is, to skilled forms of play—but to music, painting, sculpture, the dance, architecture, and so on. These are commonly called the fine arts; and literature, at least insofar as it is poetic, is to be reckoned among them. I would, however, prefer to call these the aesthetic arts, for "aesthetic" originally meant perceivable or fitted to be perceived; and the products of these arts are viewed by their creators as things essentially to be perceived—contemplated—

rather than as things to be used for practical or scientific, or for other purposes extraneous to contemplation. Moreover, the works of the decorative arts too are works of aesthetic art, at least in part, since they are intended not solely to be used but also to be contemplated.

Aesthetic art, like art of all other kinds, is a form of skilled purposive activity; the artist attempts to create an object that will satisfy certain requirements he intended it should satisfy. Accordingly, when the question is asked, "What is art?" what is called for is an account of the particular nature of these requirements; for it is their specific nature that distinguishes art in the sense of aesthetic art from the other species of art, such as engineering art, in which the aim is likewise to create some object but where success or failure is measured in terms of requirements of a different kind.

The problem of the nature of art then reduces to this question: What is the sort of consideration in the light of which the artist, as he proceeds in the creation of any one of his works, makes the many decisions he is there called upon to make—the decisions that a painter, for example, makes as to whether a line he has drawn or a color he has used is the "right" one, or is "better" or "worse" than some alternative one. The question is thus: What exactly do the words "right," "wrong," "better," "worse," mean as applied by the artist himself when judging and, if need be, correcting any one of the creative steps

he takes in the painting of a picture or in the com-
posing of a sonata, a poem, or any other work?

The most popular idea is that the artist is essentially a person who loves beauty and devotes his skill
to the creation of beautiful things; and therefore that
he corrects what he has done or lets it stand according as he judges it to detract from or contribute to
the beauty he supposedly aims at. This opinion, that
in art "right" means beautiful and "wrong" means
ugly, though at first sight plausible is nevertheless, I
believe, mistaken—except, as will be pointed out
later, in the special case of decorative as distinguished
from "free" art. It has been fostered by the common
practice of using the term "work of art" as a term
of praise—that is, in the sense of *beautiful* work of
art, instead of merely in its literal sense of product
of human skill, as distinguished from product of the
blind forces of nature. This practice, of course, automatically makes "ugly work of art" a contradiction
in adjecto.

But the practice I shall adopt instead—of meaning by a "work of art" simply a product of the form
of human activity called art—has the advantage of
not begging from the start the question as to whether
something may be a product of this activity and yet
be unbeautiful or ugly. Rather, it forces this question on our attention. I believe that, when it is fairly
faced, only an affirmative answer to it is possible.
That some paintings, for instance, are ugly things,
decidedly unpleasant to contemplate, is a fact for

which most persons will easily find corroboration in their own experience. For me to mention some that I so judge would be only to make tacitly the arrogant assumption that the reader's taste is certain to coincide with mine. But that paintings of this sort, which my suggestion brings as examples to the reader's mind, are nevertheless in many instances genuinely works of art follows from the fact that doubtless quite as much skill was required to paint them as some others—perhaps by the same artist— that are found to be beautiful, and from the further fact that the artist may well declare he achieved as successfully in them as in these others what he had aimed to do.

Of course, it might be objected that just because they are ugly they are not truly works of art; but this objection rests on no foundation other than the arbitrary use already mentioned of the term "work of art" in the sense of beautiful work of art, instead of simply in the literal sense of product of the skilled activity called art. Again, the objection might be advanced that although in some works of visual art— for example, in many of Goya's etchings—the subject represented is something ugly, yet, if they are good art, the execution—that is, the composition of lines, volumes, colors, values—is beautiful. But although there are many paintings in which ugly subject matter is redeemed by beauty of execution, it remains possible, even if uncommon, for a painter not only to pick an unpleasant subject but also to use his skill, deliberately, in making the manner of its execution likewise a source of unpleasant feelings, so that the result is ugly not only in content but also in form. Such a result, of course, will be a bad—in the sense of aesthetically displeasing—work of art, but it will be truly a work of art nonetheless if the artist's skill has been sufficient to achieve in it the effect he did intend. It is true that even in such a painting there will probably be some aspects or portions that by themselves are aesthetically pleasing; but if the artist's intent was what I have supposed it to be, then these pleasing bits will have the status of minor blunders, just as have the displeasing bits that similarly can be found in paintings where both the feelings intended to be expressed by the subject and those intended to be expressed by the manner of treatment were pleasant.

Approximate examples of such paintings would be most likely to occur among works of young artists who sometimes, in blind revolt against all tradition and bent on being original at any cost, mistake wanton iconoclasm for originality. Such systematically negative works, however skillfully they may achieve the ugliness they attempt, would, like other gratuitously unpleasant sights, have too little chance to engage attention to become known to many.

The laudatory connotation the term "work of art" commonly has come to have is probably due in large measure to the fact that the contents of museums and art galleries, which for the most part do have some beauty, are what the term first brings to mind. But these contents are not a fair sample of the products of art. On the contrary, they are a highly biased sample, for they constitute a selection of, so far as possible, the best works that have survived of the artists or periods represented; and the works themselves that have survived tend to be, not a random sample of those that were produced, but rather chiefly those that were found most beautiful and therefore were most carefully protected from destruction by the blind forces of fire, flood, war, or decay. With works of art it is as with men: the vast majority of the men we see on the streets are alive and healthy enough to be about; yet there are dead men and sick men—to be found, however, in the cemetery and the hospital, rather than on the street. Similarly, there are ugly works of art, but to find them one must look in attics, cellars, or dust bins, rather than in museums.

Beauty, thus, is to some extent a condition of the survival of a work of art. But that no intrinsic connection exists between beauty and art is sufciently proved by the fact that some works of art are not beautiful; that some things that are works, not of art but of nature, are beautiful; and that things that are works of lack of art—that is, works in which the artist's skill has confessedly been insufficient to achieve just what he intended—are nevertheless sometimes adjudged beautiful.

Aside from this, however, the hypothesis that beauty or lack of it is the criterion by which the artist, as he works, decides whether to let stand or to correct what he has done is perhaps most clearly invalidated by its untruth to the psychology of art creation. The criterion he uses is, in fact, much rather whether what he has done does or does not adequately express what he desired it to express. Except in decorative art, beauty has to art only a relation similar to the adventitious one that truth has to the statements we make. Generally, perhaps, we hope that the ideas our statements express are true—although a novel, of course, is a collection of statements most of which are in fact false and are known to be so. But in a novel, as well as elsewhere, what directly determines what we say is whether it adequately expresses what we mean. If truth were the criterion, then instead of the preceding sentence I could just as well or better have written that two plus two equals four, for this too is true and also more obvious. Similarly, if beauty were what the musician, for instance, is essentially aiming at, then there would be no reason why he should compose a nocturne, let us say, rather than a march, provided that each had as much of beauty as the other. The opinion that beauty is what the artist aims at probably is traceable in part to the widespread failure to distinguish, in art and elsewhere, between the aim of an activity and the values in terms of which the product aimed at can be appraised. But the end is one thing, and the values of the end are another. And, of course, the norms to which an activity must conform if it is to achieve a given end are yet something else.

Finally, it should be noted that beauty is notoriously relative to individual taste; indeed, it comes and goes with changes of mood, of context, and so on, even in a given individual. Accordingly, if a "work of art" were defined as "a product of human skill in which beauty was intended and achieved," we should have to say, for example, that a given painting may be a work of art if it is contemplated by a given person before lunch but perhaps not after; or that when it is beheld by two persons, one of whom finds it beautiful while the other does not, then the painting both is and is not a work of art. This, I submit, is absurd, for if a painting is in fact a product of the creative human activity called art, this fact remains forever and universally a fact. On the other hand, there is no paradox in the possibility that beauty is found in a given painting by a given person at one time but not at another, or not by another person at the same time. But when this happens to be the case, the fact should be expressed by saying just that, instead of by saying that the painting is and also is not a work of art.

Art and the Imitation of Nature

Another answer, as ancient as Plato and Aristotle, to the question, "What is art?" is that art is essentially imitation. The painter, for instance, or the sculptor, is seen to stand before some real object and to observe it carefully. One further notices that the painting or the statue he creates resembles more or less closely the object before him. And, as a spec-

tator of all this, one then finds tempting the conclusion that what the artist seeks to do is to copy or
imitate the appearance of the object he has been
observing. This conclusion is plausible, at least
superficially, in the case of the painter's or the sculptor's activity; but having once been suggested by
observation of such examples, it is rashly and forcibly
extended to the other arts. Music, for instance, is
then described as imitating the emotions, although it
is obvious that "imitating" is used in this case, arbitrarily, in the sense of inducing or expressing instead
of in the normal sense of creating an object that
resembles another object used as model. Music, of
course, is imitative in the latter sense only when its
sounds are made to resemble sounds in nature, such
as the song of birds, the crash of thunder, or the
roar of the wind.

The imitation theory of the nature of art is thus
open to the fatal objection that much of art makes no
attempt to create likenesses of objects. This is the case
with most of music; with the dance, other than pan-
tomime; with architecture; and, in graphic art, with
all abstract or purely formal design. Moreover, even
where the imitation theory is most plausible—namely,
in the case of the painter who is painting a landscape
or a portrait or a still life—the truth is that, if he is
truly an artist and not merely a human copying machine, he is then editing and interpreting his "model,"
not attempting to copy it as literally as possible.

The latter, on the contrary is what a skilled
handler of paints and brush would do who had

been commissioned to make for a private collection a faithful copy of some famous painting in a museum. To do this, great technical skill is, of course, required; but the activity is not on this account art, except in the sense in which the reproduction of the painting by skillful color photolithography would also be art. That is, it is engineering art, but not art in the sense with which we are here concerned, where freedom and exercise of the creative imagination is of the essence. To seek to reproduce as exactly as possible the appearance of an object is to seek to obtain a *document*—whether for scientific or historical or commercial purposes— or else it is only an art-school exercise by which the student acquires demonstrable control of his medium in order that, when or if he eventually has something of his own to say, he will have the technical skill to say it exactly.

Art and Play

Again, it has been supposed that art is a special form of play—play itself being conceived as vicarious expenditure of surplus energy. Labor is something undertaken under pressure of external necessity, for the sake of the practical utility of its products; but art and play seem alike in that neither creates things useful for bending man's natural environment to his welfare. Play is engaged in for the enjoyment of it; and to the spectator the same appears to be true of art, since it does not appear to perform any life-serving function. Hence it is easy to believe that art is only a particular form of play. Not only the body, however, but also the mind has its play activities, and the stream of images that flows spontaneously through a mind not bent on any specific task is conceived as the play activity of the imagination, through which it discharges the mental energy that accumulates when no external problem presents itself to exercise it.

Critics have pointed out, however, that play is often carried on to the point of exhaustion; and also that what initiates it, at least in animals, is often simply some external stimulus, as when a leaf blown by the wind starts the kitten in pursuit. Thus play is not essentially, but only accidentally, a self-initiated discharge of stored-up surplus energy. Aside from this, however, to describe as play the spontaneous flow of images through the idle mind seems rather inappropriate. It is not, like play, deliberately undertaken for the sake of enjoyment, but is rather the manifestation of a mental restlessness comparable to the bodily restlessness of the child who finds it impossible to keep still for more than a moment.

Moreover, even Friedrich Schiller, who originated the play theory of the nature of art, perceived—as Herbert Spencer, who adopted it, did not—that the spontaneous flow of images through the mind does not in itself constitute art, but that art is born only when a new power comes into exercise—the formative, controlling, purposive activity that selects, edits, supplements, and orders the images that spontaneously present themselves. Art is essentially creative, whereas play is so only by accident. Play is engaged in, not for the sake of its possible objective results, but for the sake of the enjoyment derived from exercise of the powers it employs; whereas the art-creative activity, like labor, is earnest in that its products are esteemed important by the artist, although it differs from labor in that the creation of works of art is undertaken in obedience to an inner instead of an external compulsion. And because it has this obligatory character, the art-creative activity is, like labor, carried on many times beyond the point where it ceases to be enjoyed; whereas play is abandoned as soon as such a point is reached, or, if carried beyond it, ceases to be play and becomes drudgery perhaps then altruistically performed for the sake of the partners' pleasure or for some other ulterior purpose.

Art and the Impulse to Charm

Yet another theory is that of H. R. Marshall, which stems from and improves upon Darwin's conception of art as self-display, serving as an instrument of sexual selection on an aesthetic basis. Marshall describes the art-creative impulse as an impulse to act so as to attract by pleasing—that is, by charming rather than by benefiting. This impulse, he emphasizes, is blind as to its own function. The artist is not plotting to please; he is not creating objects deliberately planned by him to be effective means of charming. The impulse that moves him indeed tends to have this result; but it is an automatic, not an intended or anticipated, result. In any case, this result is what Marshall regards as accounting for the survival of art and as pointing to the role of art in society. It is an instrument, not of sexual attraction only, but of attraction in general; and its function thus is social consolidation.

This theory, evidently, is based on the very assumption we have earlier found reasons to deny—namely, that art is a human activity whose very nature it is to produce beautiful and hence pleasing objects. The fact, however, is that some works of art are found displeasing to contemplate by some persons; and that, insofar as this is so, art then serves as an instrument, not of attraction, but of repulsion. Thus, instead of concluding as Marshall does that the function of art is social consolidation, we should have to say that its function is rather social assortment—the attracting to one another of persons of like taste or like mood, but also the driving apart of those whose tastes or emotional dispositions would conflict, so that social friction is thereby minimized. There is little doubt that this double function is indeed performed by art, but it is far from being all that art does. That art is capable of performing it is but one of the corollaries of the essential nature of art.

Aside from this, however, it should be noticed that Marshall's hypothesis, even if accepted, provides no answer to the particular question we have had in view. For it was pointed out that the question, "What essentially is art?" reduces to a question as to

what sort of consideration governs the decisions—the
judgments of right or wrong—that the artist makes
on his own work as it proceeds; and the only answer
to this that would be consonant with Marshall's
theory would be that that governing consideration
is the probable aesthetic pleasingness or displeasing-
ness to eventual beholders of what the artist has done
or proposes to do. This, of course, simply is not the
psychological fact; and Marshall himself emphasizes
this when he insists that the art instinct impels the
artist to his work "without any appreciation whatever that he is really aiming to do what shall attract
others to him." But although Marshall thus rightly
rules out that answer, he offers no other in its stead,
saying only that "the art instinct is blind in its sim-
plicity, with no end in view at all beyond the com-
pletion of its work."

What Art Is Essentially

Other unsuccessful attempts to say what differentiates art from the other forms of purposive activity
might be reviewed here, but the discussion of those
already considered has perhaps been enough to
sharpen the meaning of the problem and to provide
us with a certain perspective upon it. I therefore now
turn to what I conceive to be the true answer to our
question. *It is that art is essentially a form of language—namely, the language of feeling, mood, sentiment, and emotional attitude.* It is thus to be dis-

tinguished from the language of assertion, which is what we use to formulate opinions, information, hypotheses, and so on. That is, what occurs in art creation is that the artist finds himself emotionally stirred—whether by something he perceives at the time or by something he thinks of, or perhaps as an effect of certain obscure psychological or physiological causes—and attempts to express the feeling that inspires him by creating an object that "embodies" it.

When art is described as "the language of feeling," the fact should be emphasized that "feeling" does not here denote only the few dozen emotions and moods for which ordinary language has needed names; for otherwise this conception of art would fit only a small percentage of works of art. These feelings—love, fear, anger, jealousy, anxiety, and the rest—are only the typical feelings aroused by those few more or less stereotyped situations that present themselves again and again in the lives of men. But the emotional life of human beings includes not only all sorts of nuances, for which we have no names, of these feelings, but also innumerable other feelings that are too rare, or too subtle and evanescent, or too unimportant as drives to immediate deeds, ever to have received names of their own.

There is hardly any situation, no matter how undramatic, that does not have for us some import of feeling; and if we do not ordinarily notice it, it is only because the word "feeling" or "emotion" leads us to expect a psychological thunderclap, as it were, whereas rather a whisper is what we should then listen for. A simple line, for example, such as this ⌇⌇⌇ is not only describably different but also emotionally different from one such as this ⋀⋁⋁; and such a color contrast as that between the paper and black type ˙on this page arouses a different feeling from that which would have resulted had the type been scarlet instead of black or had each of the letters been of one of a half-dozen colors, distributed at random. That these various simple situations each stirs in us some feeling—a determinate one in each case, peculiar to the given situation and for which no specific name exists—would ordinarily escape our notice, but becomes evident as soon as we are asked to compare attentively our inner response to one with our inner response to another. The feeling aroused in these simple situations is, of course, nowhere nearly so intense or insistent as is, for instance, the feeling of anger or that of envy; but it is nonetheless unmistakable when rightly looked for.

The examples just given of simple lines and colors should make evident also another important fact commonly unrecognized, namely, that emotional import to the spectator is possessed not only by such objects as human beings, their affairs, and the instruments and settings of their purposes—that is, by what, for short, I shall call *dramatic entities*—but also by the "abstract" or formal entities—such as lines, shapes, colors, tones, and their space or time relations—of which pure *designs* consist, a pure design being a de-

sign that does not represent anything but that literally presents itself and only itself.

The emotional import of pure designs or of any
design viewed in abstraction from the dramatic objects it may happen to represent is generally of a more
austere and aloof, less throbbing or passionate, quality than that of works that represent or suggest dramatic entities. But to suppose, on this account, that
only the latter works express feelings is a profound
error. Even the most abstract designs likewise do so.
Moreover, the particular feelings that designs do express cannot be expressed otherwise than by them.
They are different feelings from those expressed by
representations of dramatic entities, and the converse
is equally true. The dogma sometimes heard that, in
paintings, the dramatic element should come from
the design, not from the dramatic objects and situations represented, voices an impossibility. Where that
appears to occur, one has ceased to attend to the design
as such and, instead, allowed some of its elements to
suggest or vaguely represent dramatic forces and relations. This is to substitute animistic interpretation—
that is, imaginative dramatization—of the design for
attention to the peculiar import of feeling which, *qua*
design, it possesses.

Thus the dogma that would exalt design as alone
of importance not only requires of design something
it cannot really do but also acts to deprive painting,
arbitrarily, of resources it does have and for which
there is not substitute—namely, the resources that

representation of dramatic entities provides. For, once more, what can be expressed in this way cannot be expressed in any other way; and surely to apply such epithets as "illustration" or "narrative" or "literary" to paintings that avail themselves of these particular resources is not to give a reason why what they do thereby express should not be expressed. If these epithets are meant to imply that what is here done with paint could have been done better, or indeed done at all, with words, then they imply something patently false. No better example of this could be cited than Walter Pater's famous words on the "Mona Lisa." They are indeed themselves a noble example of literary art, but obviously in no way are they a substitute for the painting itself. *No art can express exactly what another art does. Not even two works of the same art can express exactly the same thing.* In the language of thought, the words of which owe their import to convention, there is such a thing as two differently worded statements that mean exactly the same thing; but in the language of feeling, which art is, there are no synonymous expressions.

The Objectification of Feeling

That art is the language of feeling and a work of art the expression in objective form of some feeling experienced by the artist was argued in 1882 by Eugène Véron, in a book entitled *L'Esthétique,* seldom read today. Its main theses have become known chiefly through Tolstoi, who makes them the basis of his own book, *What Is Art?* but who conceives language as being communication—transmission from one man to another—rather than, as Véron does, essentially expression. The difference is perhaps of no great practical importance; but in support of my agreement on this point with Véron rather than Tolstoi, I may point out that, without expression first, there could be no transmission. Transmission is something that, when it occurs, occurs through exhibition of the product of expression. Language thus, whether it be language of assertion or language of feeling, is at least expression. On the other hand, once objective expression has taken place, transmission depends on factors —such as the presence and attention of spectators, and their capacity for the thought or the feeling expressed—that are, for the most part, not within the control of the writer or the artist; or whose control of these factors, so far as he may have and exercise it, is an activity distinct both in kind and in motive from his activity *qua* writer or artist. Like other human beings, he no doubt does not like to be alone in his opinions or in what he feels; but the activities to which this leads him—of which the display of his works is but one—are manifestations of his gregarious impulse, not of his creative impulse. The latter has no ulterior ends, although indeed its products can be and are turned to all sorts of ends.

Objective expression, in the case of the language of feeling, means substantially the same thing as in the language of assertion. When we do what is called "putting our thought into words," we do not put it in in the literal sense in which we put water into a bucket. What we do is to create an object—specifically, a sentence—in which the thought is "embodied" or "objectified," in the sense that from it, by reading, the thought that dictated the words can be recovered. Similarly, in the case of art, objective expression of a feeling means that an object is created—an arrangement of color shapes perhaps, or of tones, and so on—from which, through contemplation, can be obtained back the feeling of which that object is itself the expression. The faithfulness with which the object reflects that feeling is the measure of the adequacy with which it has been objectified.

Expression that is objective in this sense differs from expression that is a merely impulsive blowing off of emotional steam, in that the products of the latter do not have the capacity to reflect back—to instigate in the beholder—the feeling that gave rise to them. The words and gestures of two men quarreling, for instance, inform us that they are angry, but do not make us share their anger. On the other hand, an expression of anger that is a work of art, as by an actor on the stage, can reproduce in a spectator capable of it the feeling embodied by the playwright in the actor's part.

The description of a work of art as the objectification of a feeling would be open to serious criticism if it were taken to mean that the rich and complex feeling that some elaborate work finally embodies was present from the very start in the mind of the artist, who had then nothing left to do but construct the object adequate to express it. With rare exceptions, this is the artist's problem only as regards each of the innumerable small steps through which the work eventually comes to its final form. The feeling that initially inspires the artist to begin a particular work is best thought of as a seed, so to speak, of the total feeling ultimately expressed. The latter is present in the former only in the sense of being the final unfoldment of the specific potentialities—the natural proliferation—of that particular initial feeling.

What, in the great majority of cases, actually takes place is that the initial feeling moves the artist to some relatively simple creative acts; that he then contemplates the result of these acts; that out of this there arises a growth of his feeling that inspires him to certain additional creative strokes; that he then again contemplates what he has so far done; and so on, over and over again until the work attains its final form. Each creative step is inspired in part by contemplation of the result of those already taken, but is also severely restricted by them. They both demand from *him* a certain next step and forbid *him* certain conceivable others that would perhaps be possible or necessary for someone else who should take on the work at the point reached. Rousseau, we read, felt impelled to "finish" Cézanne's pictures; but had he done so, the product would have been, not a more adequate expression of the feeling that inspired Cézanne, but an expression of the different feeling inspired in Rousseau by contemplation of Cézanne's picture.

Decorative Art Distinguished from Free Art

Véron holds—and Tolstoi after him—that art in general cannot be defined as "an activity aiming at the creation of beautiful objects." He insists that art can include, not only the serene beauty typical of Greek art, but also the terrible, the sad, the ugly, the joyous, and indeed the expression of any other feelings. But he rightly perceives that there is a species of art—namely, decorative art—that is marked by the fact that, in it, beauty is deliberately or instinctively sought.

The works of the decorative arts make up an important and very large portion of the art of mankind. In the last chapter, we shall examine the anatomy of one of these—the cosmetic art—which is perhaps the most widely practised and certainly one of the most interesting among them. That it—or, more generally, decorative art—can be as truly art in the sense we have defined as can the "free" arts might be doubted by some. It will therefore be well at this point to say something to make the matter clear, and to clarify also the closely related question as to how or whether ulterior and external purposes in the artist are compatible with the creative freedom that is a *sine qua non* of all art of self-expression.

One of the characters that mark off decorative from other kinds of aesthetic art is that *the material it operates on consists of objects having some practical function to perform*. Some of the features of a work of decorative art thus are prescribed *ab initio* by the

practical function of the object. Hence they constitute restrictions within which the artist must work.
For example, in a piece of sculpture intended to function as a book end, this function requires that the
object shall have great enough mass and stability to
resist the sidewise push of a row of books, and that the
object shall remain within certain limits of size. This
means that the sculptor's creative freedom is restricted in these respects, as compared with what it
would have been if the object had been intended, not
for practical use, but only for contemplation.

It should be noticed, however, that even in the latter case some limitations would have remained. Size,
for example, would have been limited still, by such
considerations as cost of material, difficulties of trans-
portation of very large blocks, and so on; and shape,
by the properties of the particular material employed.
For some shapes are possible in bronze or in wood
that perhaps would not be so in marble. Similarly,
even the "free" painter is limited—for instance, by
the fact that the range of brightness of his pigments
is much narrower than that of the colors of nature;
and hence that, of the color effects he can imagine
and might wish to achieve, some are beyond the possibilities of his medium.

The fact is that all freedom is freedom in a jail of
some kind. Some jails are roomier than others, and
not all jail walls are made of stone; but walls there
are always. To say that freedom is ever limited, however, is not to say there is none, nor that what there
is of it within the limits of each situation is not gen-

uine. Indeed, the limits themselves can sometimes be taken as opportunities and function as sources of inspiration. That the works of decorative art are not only objects to be contemplated, but also have to serve one or another sort of practical instrumentality, is thus only one more limitation in addition to those within which have to work even the arts that are "free" in the sense of seeking for themselves the maximum possible of freedom. In respect to freedom, then, the difference between decorative and "free" art is but one of degree.

Another character, which is of the essence of decorative art but not of art in general, is that *its products shall be aesthetically pleasing*—that is, shall have more or less of beauty. This means that, of the variety of feelings that may compete for expression in the decorative artist's mind at the time he confronts the opportunity that inspires them, he must reject any that are unpleasant and therefore such that their objective embodiments would be unbeautiful. That he must do this, however, is but an additional restriction on his creative freedom. It is not complete negation of it, any more than were the other limitations of it already mentioned.

The decorative artist retains considerable freedom even within all these boundaries. The beautiful object he finally creates is the embodiment of feelings that genuinely moved him and that he sought to express; and the selection it represents from among the other objects he might have created instead, in response to the opportunity he faced, is truly an expres-

sion of his individual taste. Taste is intuition of differences of degree in the beauty of things—that is, in
the pleasingness of the feelings one experiences or
would experience in aesthetic contemplation of one
thing as compared with another. And the essence of
the decorative artist's activity is creative expression of
his own taste, in this sense of the word.

The heights decorative art, as so conceived, can
reach may be seen in some of the Oriental lacquers
and ivories, in some of the pieces of modern or ancient glass, in some of Cellini's work, and in many
other objects made by craftsmen who happened to be
gifted artists in their own media. A particularly interesting contemporary example is to be found in the
arrangements of paintings in groups with pieces of
furniture and other objects of distinguished crafts-
manship in the gallery of the Barnes Foundation.
The color photographs of some of these groups, which
have been published, are sufficient to show that the
works of decorative art these arrangements themselves
constitute may well be ranked in aesthetic merit with
some of the objects out of which they are composed.

When no freedom at all remains to the artist, art,
conceived as objectification of feelings that move him,
automatically ceases. If he nevertheless creates something, he is then creating only in the sense in which
skilled manufacture or, more generally, the various
engineering arts create. That is, in both instances the
characters given to the object created are prescribed
at every point from the outside—by certain functions
the object is to perform or by desiderata, not the mak-

er's own, the object is to meet. If, for example, the sculptor's decisions are dictated, not by what he feels impelled to express or by his own taste, but by what he thinks the public will like, then he is simply a skilled manufacturer of aesthetic candy, catering, as do the makers of chocolate bars or of ice cream, to the prevailing taste of their prospective buyers.

Again, if a painter, commissioned to paint the view from the terrace of some estate, is governed at every step in what he puts on the canvas by the comments and directions of his patron standing at his elbow, then the painter functions only as a painting machine, of which the push buttons are operated by the patron; for it is the latter's inspiration or taste, such as it may be, and not the painter's own that are then being expressed. Only insofar as the requirements of the commission are elastic enough to leave him some freedom of self-expression can the painter function truly as an artist, instead of merely as a skilled and obedient handler of brush and pigment.

Another example worth mentioning in the present connection is that of love poems, which, it has often been pointed out, have in perhaps most instances been written in the hope of winning the beloved's favor. Since this is an ulterior, external purpose, are such poems then genuinely art? The answer is that if the feelings exressed in the poem do not honestly depict the poet's heart, but are any he thinks likely to move the particular woman he believes his beloved to be, then the poem is art only in the sense in which fly fishing for trout is an art—that is, the poet's activity is then a species of engineering: seducement engineering. But if, on the contrary, the sentiments the poet expresses are ones he truly feels, then the fact that he also hopes they will, when displayed, arouse love for him in the heart of his lady in no way implies that his activity as he writes the poem is not genuinely art.

When, in a later chapter, we come to examine the art of personal fascination, we shall need to keep in mind the remarks made here on decorative art and on the subject of ulterior ends in the artist's mind. They will enable us to distinguish between the conditions under which the cosmetic art is art in the sense of creative expression of taste and those under which it is but a particular species of engineering art.

Every Man Naturally an Artist

Even when analysis is correct, it is of the very nature of it to present us with something that looks different from what we undertook to analyze. We might find it hard, for example, to recognize even our own brother if he were exhibited to us after having been subjected to careful anatomical dissection. Similarly, our analysis of the art-creative activity as skilled objectification of feeling may have had the effect of making this activity seem an unfamiliar one, reserved for a relatively few specially gifted persons. The truth, however, is much rather that, virtually, all of us engage in it on many occasions, even if at a humble level. They are chiefly the occasions on which, in the course of ordinary life, we express our taste creatively. The adornment of our bodies or the styling of their appearance are perhaps the most obvious examples. The dressing of the hair on head and face or the selection of clothing and jewelry may follow more or less closely the fashions of the day, but even then it involves numerous choices—as between colors, fabrics, patterns, available styles, and so on—that are made by the individual in accordance with his taste and that express it. This is true also of the selection and arrangement of the furnishings of our homes or of the designing of our gardens. Indeed, even our behavior can be, and often is, for us a field for creative expression of our taste. It becomes so whenever we undertake—as all but the smuggest of us sometimes do—to edit our own manners, forms of speech, intonations, handwriting, and gestures to a form that will accord more closely with our taste and with what we feel ourselves really to be, than they did before it occurred to us to observe them critically.

If such activities are often not recognized as forms of art, it is only because, like the handicrafts in the days before machine production, they are so familiar; whereas art, in the minds of many, has come to be thought of as something more or less esoteric, which occurs only in studios and employs less common media. Even as regards arts of the latter sort, however, most of us have some capacity for them; for the language of feeling is not inherently more difficult than the language of thought.

What is difficult and therefore rare is consummate mastery of either. Moreover, just as, among persons who have learned to write, only a few have original or profound thoughts to set forth, so, among those who have developed a degree of capacity to express themselves in some technical art medium, not many have novel or important feelings to express. Most of the paintings, for example, to be seen at exhibitions are on about the same level of originality or importance as are the themes or term papers handed in by students in college classes. There was a time when only a very few people were able to write; and, because of the rarity of their attainment, they were then regarded—irrespective of what they did write, and much as artists are today—as beings especially gifted. Yet the fact, then as now, is that almost everyone else, with a little training and application, could also have learned to write. Likewise, most people today could acquire the similarly modest control of some technical art medium that is all that was needed, for instance, to paint most of the paintings we see.

Art, thus, is no abnormal growth on the tree of human life; nor is it an adventitious ornament tacked on to it here and there. It is essentially a branch of language, and as natural and normal a human activity as skilled speech. From this, its essence, flows art's capacity for the various functions it performs that give it its human importance.

From the standpoint of the artist himself, one of these functions is to serve as the most effective means of relieving the emotional tension that goes with the artistic temperament—the temperament, namely, in which feelings are stirred more easily and more intensely than in most persons by colors, shapes, sounds, and other situations, whether perceived or imagined, to which one is related as spectator, not as participant.

But in addition to providing him this relief, and more importantly, creation provides the artist with a mirror of the feeling aspect of his soul, through which its movements, until then obscure, reach clarity for him. This, as already suggested, affords him opportunity for study, criticism, and emendation of that aspect of himself. But it also makes possible for him novel, more subtle feeling intuitions—just as, once we have succeeded in putting an idea exactly and clearly into words, reflection upon it then becomes possible; and new insights, that were impossible until the idea was clear, now become possible.

Another function of art, as already pointed out, is to serve human beings as a means of acquaintance with one another's horizons of feeling. Art so functions not only as between the artist and those to whom he shows his works, but also, and much more widely, as between the beholders themselves of his works. For the comments made by one of them to another concerning a picture, poem, musical composition, or piece of architecture that both know quickly reveal to both whether or not harmony of taste, sentiment, mood, and emotional attitude subsists between them. Art, moreover, because it provides an objective and therefore public record of the aesthetic insights of many of the most sensitive and aesthetically probing men, furnishes us with invaluable implements of aesthetic education; for, as will be pointed out at greater length farther on, works of art are to aesthetic education what scientific treatises and other records of information already won are to intellectual education.

CHAPTER III

THE APPRECIATION OF ART

IN THE PRECEDING CHAPTER, we considered art from the standpoint of the creator of works of art. Now we pass to the standpoint of the man I have proposed to call the "consumer" of the work created by the artist. He is the ordinary man who hangs on the walls of his room pictures he likes; who, from time to time, goes to concerts or tunes his radio to some music program; who occasionally reads poetry, visits a museum, looks at cathedrals, or goes to the theater to see a play or a ballet.

More particularly, however, the standpoint I now wish to examine is that of the consumer insofar as his interest in the works of art he contemplates is the aesthetic interest, as distinguished from, for instance, the historical or the commercial interest, or the religious, the ethical, the psychological, or other interest. Accordingly, the ordinarily rather broad term "contemplation" will here be used in the more specific sense of *aesthetic* contemplation; and the term "consumer," similarly, to mean the person interested in the specifically aesthetic "consumption" of works of art or of other possible objects of this interest.

Of the works of art to which he gives his attention, the ordinary consumer likes some, dislikes others, and likes certain ones better than certain others; but he has no pretensions to being what is called a critic. He does not claim that these judgments of his on the works of art he contemplates are authoritative. Rather, he usually is ready—indeed, I think, too ready—to concede that very possibly they are wrong; for he has no clear idea of the sense attached in this connection to the word "wrong" by the critic who would apply it to those judgments of his, and he is conscious that he would be able to say but little, if anything, in support of them.

The question into which we must now look is this: What exactly is to be understood by the description, as aesthetic, of the interest that animates him? What precisely is the nature of the attitude, sometimes called the aesthetic attitude, with which he approaches works of art?

Although much has been written about it, this attitude is not particularly mysterious. It consists in attention to a work of art—or indeed to any other object—insofar as the attention is combined with interest exclusively in the import of feeling that the object then has for the person who faces it. That is, the beholder approaches it, as it were, with the questions, "What does it make me feel? What sensations, sentiments, or mood does it arouse in me?" instead of with the more common sorts of interest that would be represented by the questions: "What is to be done about it? What is it good for?" or "What accounts for it? What is it a sign of?"

Aesthetic contemplation, thus, might be described as *a "listening" for the feeling impact—for the emotive reverberations—of the object attended to.* Aesthetic response to a color, for example, does not consist in recognizing or classifying it, or in interpreting it as a sign of something or other, but in *savoring* it—just as an ordinary person simply savors the aroma of a cigar or the bouquet of a wine, whereas a professional taster might rather *use* the aroma or the flavor as an indication of the article's species, origin, or age. The aesthetic attitude, that is, presupposes the inhibiting of inquisitiveness and of interest in the practical bearings of the object upon concerns of ours extraneous to that object itself. It consists, instead, in throwing ourselves open to whatever nuances of sensation, emotion, or mood the object attended to is capable of causing in us. In this respect, aesthetic contemplation is to feelings what looking for is to possible sights, what sniffing is to possible odors, or what listening for is to possible sounds. But since there is in the language no generic verb meaning simply "to make oneself receptive to" (without specifying to what), our only recourse here is to borrow, as I did above, one of the specific verbs such as "listening for" and to use it in quotations as generic in this particular connection.

From this account of the consumer's attitude, it is evident that aesthetic contemplation is the exact psy-

chological converse of the artist's creative activity.
The artist attempts to express the feeling that inspires him at the time by creating something that, in
the sense already considered, will objectify or embody the feeling. The aesthetic consumer's attempt,
on the other hand, is to extract from the object the
feeling it embodies—the feeling, if the object be a
work of art, that was put into it by the artist; or, if
the object be a work of nature, the feeling of which
it is the natural vehicle. For, as already pointed out,
there is no object, whether simple or complex, man-
made or natural, visual or auditory, that does not
have its own capacity to excite in the contemplative
beholder feelings or nuances of feeling different from
those that any distinguishably different object would
excite. Indeed, the fact that objects do have this capacity is what makes it possible for them to be the vo-
cabulary, as it were, of the language of the artist, who,
through appropriate selection and combination of
objects, finds it possible to express the specific feeling that inspires him at a given time.

Aesthetic contemplation, then, is to artistic creation what impression is to expression, what deliberately adopted receptiveness is to deliberate and con-
trolled pouring out. It is the exact analogue, in the
language of feeling, of what in the language of
thought is called reading—that is, of the attempt to
extract from somebody else's words the ideas, opinions, or information he expressed in them.

Having now clearly in mind what aesthetic contemplation is, let us next ask what conditions are favorable or unfavorable to it.

Aids and Hindrances to Contemplation

For an animal, to have the things needed to maintain life and a modicum of bodily and mental comfort is enough to justify living. But for man, it is only the foundation indispensable to a truly human life. When his animal needs are insured, his surplus of time and energy is turned by him to the pursuits that mark him off from all other living things—to art and contemplation, science, religion, and so on. To man, as distinguished from the animal in which he dwells, these alone are self-justifying in the sense of being worth while, irrespective of such biological utility as they may happen also to have.

Yet because the existence—first and throughout—of that animal foundation is a *sine qua non* of the later more fragile cultural superstructure, the impulses that, like the contemplative, generate the superstructure but contribute little or nothing directly to its biological base are in most men less alert and less strong than those that built and keep up that base. These are the practical impulse—interest in what is to be *done* with or about any situation one faces— and the pragmatically inquisitive impulse—*curiosity* directed by existing but not immediately pressing aims. It is with these that the interest in aesthetic contemplation has to compete; and, since ordinarily it cannot match their strength, it only gains the chance to manifest itself in situations that do not arouse them or where they have already been satisfied.

Situations likely not to arouse these impulses or to do so but weakly would be, for example, foreign scenes as seen by a tourist or historical scenes visited in imagination that have been robbed by the centuries of practical bearing on the hopes and fears of today. Thus it is that beauty is easier to see abroad than at home. Distance, whether in space or time, or both, is the typical bar to practical participation in events. Hence the fitness of the term "psychical distance," which some psychologists have used in describing the characteristics of aesthetic contemplation. But the needed detachment from curiosity and from action is often easy also toward such natural objects as flowers, crystals, seashells, and bird songs; and toward pure non-representative designs. It is achieved also, of course, toward paintings that represent persons or objects of human use, whenever contemplation of such paintings is truly aesthetic.

If, however, a painting that is wholly or essentially a design is given as title the name of some familiar thing—for instance, the title "Bird" or "Man, reading" —then curiosity is at once stimulated in the beholder. The title sets for him right away the problem of finding the bird or the man that is not there at all; or that, being quite inessential to the intent of a painting of this kind, is at most barely suggested by this or that line in the design. The beholder is thus virtually compelled to view the painting as one does the puzzle pictures that appear, with cross-word puzzles and other such games, in the Sunday editions of the newspapers; and this, it may be assumed, is the last thing the artist really desired. The use of such misleading titles is thus simply a psychological blunder, inhibiting as it does aesthetic contemplation until the riddle forced on the beholder has been solved by him or given up in disgust. The title should serve much rather to satisfy at once such curiosity as may spontaneously arise in him as to what the artist was attempting to paint, so that nothing then remains to hinder the beholder's aesthetic interest in the painting.

Examples both of appropriately titled paintings and of others whose titles, for reasons such as those mentioned, are inapt, may be found in almost any collection of reproductions that includes some modern paintings. Thus, at the end of T. M. Greene's *The Arts and the Art of Criticism,* for instance, the title "Abstraction" is obviously fitting for each of the two paintings, by Kandinsky and Picasso, reproduced on pages 562 and 563; as is "Composition in Black, White, and Red" for Mondrian's composition, also reproduced there. On the other hand, in the case of the painting by Macdonald-Wright, reproduced on page 300 of W. H. Wright's *Modern Painting,* it would have been better to have left the word "Arm" out of the title "Arm Organisation in Blue-Green," since nothing recognizable as an arm is evident in it. Similarly, the title "Hiéroglyphe Dynamique du Bal Tabarin," for Severini's painting on page 274, has the defect of tempting the beholder to try to discover in it shapes of things that would be seen in a dance hall. Whether or not a diligent search would reveal any, the fact remains that interest in hunting for them is something radically different from the interest in aesthetic contemplation that the painting presumably was intended to receive and for which the way would have been left clear if it had been titled, let us say, simply "Composition Dynamique."

Remarks analogous to those concerning titles that set an intellectual problem to the spectator would apply to what is called program music. When a listener is told of some series of non-musical events, the perceiving or imagining of which inspired in the composer the feelings his music expresses, the listener is then in effect being invited, not to listen to the music as such, but to engage instead in the intellectual game of guessing which of those events is the one that inspired this or that part of the music.

If a painting is intended to represent at all objects of familiar kinds, this is or should be because the import of feeling the particular objects do have is a part of the feeling the artist attempted to express. In such a case, therefore, psychological common sense demands that the objects concerned be represented unambiguously enough not to arouse curiosity as to what they are supposed to be. Again, if a painting should happen to represent a man, sword in hand, in an attitude of attack, what he is attacking should be included in the picture and not left to speculation, since to arouse speculation is automatically to inhibit contemplation. Artists, naturally, desire that their works be noticed; but again and again the devices they use to invite attention indicate failure on their part to realize that the sort of attention obtained by these devices is not the contemplative attention they really desire for their works. As just pointed out, appeals to curiosity defeat this desire, as do appeals to loathing, disgust, anger, lust, or other violent emotions if the emotion is aroused so strongly that, instead of being savored, it is immediately discharged in action—inducing the beholder, for example, to turn away from the shocking or repulsive or fearful sight presented to him. Ugliness, similarly, penalizes and therefore discourages aesthetic contemplation. Beauty, on the contrary, rewards and encourages it. There is no sort of feeling that art may not express; but the feelings called the passions, since they are powerful drives to immediate action, can be touched upon by art only lightly if contemplation is not *ab initio* to be rendered impossible.

Among devices that, on the contrary, inhibit impulses to action and thereby invite contemplation may be mentioned the effective physical separation of the theater stage from the audience. For if the actors were enacting the play instead virtually among the spectators, the impulse for the latter to take part in the action of the play could easily become strong enough to win them from the contemplative attitude. Again, the frames in which pictures are put have the effect automatically of placing the pictures for us in a category different from that of the objects around them, which we normally do not contemplate but only recognize and use.

There is another device that is highly effective but is not, like those mentioned, external to the work. Rather, it is an intrinsic and important part of it; since, in addition to facilitating contemplation, it is itself one of the sources of aesthetic values in the work. I refer to what, in painting, is known as composition and, in literature, as style. Herbert Spencer's essay on the philosophy of style is founded—and, I believe, rightly—on the premise that goodness of style is a matter of economy of the reader's attention. This itself results from the intelligent use of a variety of means at the writer's disposal—from the choice, for example, of a long or short word, according to the nature of the occasion; or of one way of ordering the parts of a sentence in preference to another way; and, to a large extent, from care by the writer to make clear what logical connection there is between his successive sentences. The language provides him with such connectives as "for," "hence," "but," "on the other hand," and the like; and when, with regard to each statement, he has taken the trouble to make plain, by means of them, whether it is offered as a reason for the statement that precedes or as a conclusion from it, or as a possible objection to it, or as an illustration of what the preceding one described, or as an additional item in a description, or as a summary of matters detailed before, and so on—then the reader's attention, instead of being strained and perhaps wandering or going astray, is, as it were, taken by the hand and led by the author at each moment where it should go.

In a painting, the composition—the arrangement of lines, planes, volumes, lights and darks, colors, and so on—can similarly be used as a guide to the beholder's attention, turning it away from directions irrelevant to intuition of what the artist intended to express and along those helpful for this. Furthermore, just as in literature a style that is good in the sense described not only makes reading easy but is itself one important source of pleasure in the reading of what it renders easy to read, so in painting good composition, in the same sense, both makes a picture easy to see and adds positive aesthetic value of its own to the aesthetic value that may be possessed by what it makes us see.

On the other hand, to claim, as some would nowadays, that only composition and its intrinsic aesthetic values are of real importance and that the nature of the objects represented has no relevance to the proper aims of painting is a blunder similar to that which, in literature, would consist in claiming that what a book says is not important but only, or above all, that it should say it well.

Other Forms of Interest in Works of Art

In what precedes, we have considered the consumer of art only insofar as his interest is the aesthetic interest, for it is only then that his approach to works of art is relevant to the artist's attempt to express objectively the feeling that moved him. That is, only through aesthetic contemplation of a work of art does the beholder have the chance to get out of the work the feeling the artist put into it. Even then, of course, the chance that he will get it exactly and fully is relatively small. For the artist judged the object he had created adequate when, in contemplation of it, he found that the feeling he had intended to express was faithfully induced again *in him;* but since the psychological constitution of any other beholder is more or less different from his, it is not unlikely that the feeling induced in someone else by contemplation of the given work will be somewhat different from the feeling it induces in the artist himself.

But, aside from this, it is quite possible and legitimate that the interest with which a particular beholder approaches works of art or a given work of art should be, not the aesthetic interest, but some other—for example, interest in the practical bearings of the work on religion, or on public morals, or on social reform, or on some other subject. William James says somewhere that "the good thing about a work of art is that it tells all sorts of things to different spectators, of none of which things the artist ever knew a word." Whether it is indeed *the* good thing or *a* good thing might be disputed, but there is at least no doubt that it is a fact. And if one were to judge it a deplorable fact, this could, so far as I can see, only be on the ground that the expressions of language ought never to be treated otherwise than as instruments of communication and ought to be evaluated solely in terms of the degree of efficiency with which they serve this purpose. But this obviously would be as bigoted a pronouncement and as senseless a piece of intolerance as would, for instance, be the assertion that gold ought not to be used for jewelry or in any way other than as a medium of exchange, or that soybeans ought not to be used as material for plastics but only as food.

We all have heard the anecdote of the girl to whom, of an evening, her self-supposed soulmate was expounding his deepest thoughts, but who, when at last he paused, expecting her to express agreement with them, only looked up adoringly and murmured how musical and soothing was his voice. The disappointment and loneliness of discovering that others did not find the pearls we had meant to cast before them has at least cosmic compensation whenever they find in our offerings pearls we did not ourselves suspect were there.

That these remarks have a special pertinence to literature will be made clear by a few words concerning the peculiar position it occupies among the other arts. "Literature," considered etymologically, means anything written, and thus applies not only to the *Iliad,* Plato's *Republic,* and Shakespeare's works, but also to dime novels and even to the mail-order catalogue and the telephone directory. This forces us to ask whether the latter, too, are works of art, or at least are such in the same sense of the word "art" as are the former.

Our analysis of aesthetic art, it will be recalled,

revealed its essence as consisting in skilled objective expression of feeling. It is the language of feeling; and occasion arose more than once to compare it with the language of conceptual thought, which is the skilled expression in words of assertions, questions, suppositions. Because the latter also is a skilled activity, it too is art, and indeed art of self-expression; but because what is expressed here is essentially thought or knowledge instead of feeling, it should be described as logical rather than aesthetic art, or better perhaps as *lectical* art, since the adjective "logical," as most commonly used, would tend to suggest falsely that expression only of reasonings is concerned.

Now there is literature in which expression of thoughts or of knowledge is the essential intent, and where any feelings that the reading might happen to excite would be unintended and irrelevant to the writer's purpose. The telephone directory or a scientific treatise would exemplify literature of this essentially didactic sort. But there is also literature in which (as in paintings that represent objects or persons and their relations) thoughts or facts are stated, or situations are described, not for their own sakes, but because of the import of feeling possessed by them or by the images they arouse—the feeling being what the writer was essentially concerned to express. This would be the case especially in lyric poetry; but also, in greater or less degree, in all other forms of literature intended to have dramatic or pictorial import, whether it be intended or not to have also didactic import. The novel, the story, and the drama suggest themselves in this connection, as well as epic poetry. Thus a great deal of literature has to be described as "mixed art"—as partly aesthetic, its product insofar an object for aesthetic contemplation; and partly lectical, its product insofar an object for assent, dissent, or doubt. Moreover, in verse, in prose poems, and, to some extent also, in much of other prose, feeling is intended to be expressed, not only through the intermediary of the thoughts formulated or of the images generated by the words, but also directly by the musical features of the language used—tempo, rhythm, rhyme, assonance, alliteration, and so on.

But aesthetic contemplation and the intellectual interest resulting in assent, dissent, or doubt are not the only possible modes of approach to literary compositions. For example, some stories—such as many mystery, detective, or picaresque novels—have little or no didactic or aesthetic intent, but appeal and are intended to appeal essentially to the desire for entertainment. They are works of the art of entertainment; and, for their readers, they are a species of spectator sport that provides excitement through vicarious adventure.

The fact is that literature is the most versatile of all means of representation. There is no aspect of nature, of human relations, or of human thought or experience that it cannot in some measure represent; and it therefore has potentially all the dimensions of interest that life itself has. But it has, in addition, all the resources of the creative imagination.

In this chapter, we have sought to make clear what constitutes aesthetic contemplation of a work of art or of nature. We have seen that it could well be said to consist in the "aesthetic reading" of such works, since it is the exact analogue in the case of the language of feeling of what "reading" is in the case of the language of assertion. We examined next some of the factors that make aesthetic contemplation easy or difficult. And we then pointed out that it is possible and quite legitimate to seek in works of art values of kinds other than aesthetic—that is, to value them otherwise than in terms of beauty, although beauty is doubtless what the consumer generally values most in them.

We have not so far attempted to say just what beauty itself is, but have been content to depend in the use we have made of the term on the intuitive apprehension everyone has of its meaning. The time has now come, however, when we must try to analyze it. This will be the task of the next chapter.

CHAPTER IV

BEAUTY IN ART AND NATURE

Beauty, or even the thought of it, is a thing so mysteriously thrilling to many persons that they regard as both sacrilege and presumption any attempt to dissect it, feeling that this but kills instead of reveals its pure essence. To them, as to a man describing his beloved, only lyrical terms can do justice to the precious thing.

An account of beauty in terms of this kind, however, does not enable us to deal with the paradoxes that seem to hedge it about, nor to distinguish it clearly from other nearly allied categories of aesthetic value. For this, what we have to have is an analysis of its nature and its sources as dispassionate and precise as alone serves in cases where the thing analyzed is of a more prosaic sort. Of course, that even the most exact analysis of beauty will not do for us what concrete beauty itself does is to be granted. But the converse of this holds equally, and in the present connection the analysis is what we need and will now undertake.

One of the most notorious facts about beauty is its variability. One man finds beauty where another finds none; and, indeed, one man may judge drab today what yesterday he judged beautiful, or beautiful today what tomorrow he will find drab or even perhaps ugly. Again, a color we find beautiful in a certain object strikes us as ugly in some other. We find blue eyes beautiful, perhaps, but not so a blue nose. Probably it is this variability with person, time, and context that, as much as anything else, has raised the question as to whether beauty is objective or subjective—whether it is a quality intrinsic to certain objects but that only some persons can perceive, and these only sometimes; or whether, on the contrary, it is a peculiar state of consciousness sometimes caused by certain objects in some of us but not in others, or not at other times.

After a little reflection, however, it becomes evident that neither hypothesis is really tenable. Let us consider, first, the objective hypothesis; and, in doing so, let us bear in mind the often neglected fact that not only is beauty to be accounted for but also its opposite, ugliness, and also the intermediate character of being neither beautiful nor ugly but aesthetically indifferent or neutral, that we may call drabness.

If now, adhering to the objective view of beauty, I say of a given thing which I find beautiful that the beauty I find in it is a quality intrinsic to the thing, but that some persons lack the eye to see it, it is obvious that such a person may then similarly assert that the drabness or perhaps positive ugliness which *he* finds in the thing is really in it, but that I lack the eye to see it. Both assertions have a certain plausibility so long as he and I are not attending strictly to the same part or aspect of the thing. But if this source of misunderstanding is done away with through choice of a sufficiently simple thing to observe, or in some other way, and yet he finds it unbeautiful and I beautiful, then it follows that really the same thing (not two different parts of the same thing) is both beautiful and ugly, or both beautiful and drab. But, of course, this is paradoxical; for ugliness and drabness are characters just as categorical as beauty, and they preclude it just as it precludes them. The case is thus not of the innocuous sort where I see something and the other person simply fails to see it; but is one where, instead of what I see, he sees something categorically incompatible with what I see.

It is to avoid this paradox that the subjective hypothesis is resorted to that supposes beauty to be, not an absolute quality resident in the object, but a certain feeling caused in the beholding subject by the object. The minds of two persons, the argument goes, are more or less differently constituted, and the mind of even one person is in a more or less different condition at different times; and it is just as natural that the same object should affect differently minds that are different as it is that the same tepid water should feel warm to a hand that is cold but cool to a hand that is hot.

This hypothesis grants that beauty or ugliness depends *in part* on the nature of the object, but insists that it is also partly dependent on the nature of the response of the contemplating subject—more specifically, on the pleasure or displeasure caused in him by contemplation of the object. But the error, which alone and gratuitously labels the hypothesis subjective, comes when this dependence of beauty on the pleasure of the beholder is described by saying that beauty is a state or activity or feeling of the mind that contemplates the object, not a property of the object that causes the feeling. This is true, not of beauty, but of pleasure; not of ugliness, but of displeasure. When anyone says, "This sunset is beautiful," what he is speaking *about* undoubtedly is the sunset he sees, *not* his own mind or its feelings; but what he is *asserting* about that sunset by declaring it beautiful is that *it* has the property or capacity of causing pleasure in him when he contemplates it.

Evidently, then, there is no paradox in the fact that one person may find beautiful the same sunset another person finds perhaps raw or garish or drab; for the same sunset well may have the capacity to cause pleasure in one contemplative beholder and displeasure or indifference in another beholder who is differently constituted—just as water, for example, has the capacity to extinguish burning wood and also the capacity to activate burning magnesium.

The question whether beauty is objective or subjective is thus not answerable by saying simply "yes" to one and "no" to the other of the alleged alternatives. The only correct answer is that *beauty is that property of an object which consists in capacity of the object to cause pleasure in a subject who contemplates it.* Beauty, that is to say, is a character of some objects, but a *relational* character of them—the character, namely, that consists in their having to certain minds (subjects) the relation just described. The question whether beauty is objective or subjective is thus exactly parallel logically with the question whether poisonousness is objective or subjective.

The account we have given of the nature of beauty, it should be noticed, accords not only with the notorious variability of judgments of beauty and their relativity to the taste and mood of the judging individual, but also with the common-sense opinion that there is no paradox in supposing that something that one finds beautiful is beautiful even when he no longer looks at it or when nobody looks at it. For this is true in the same sense in which it is true that arsenic is poisonous even when nobody swallows it— arsenic being at *all* times such that *if* one were to swallow it in certain quantity, it would cause one to die. What is false is not that arsenic is at all times poison*ous*, but that it is at all times poison*ing*. Experiencing pleasure, like dying, is not a capacity but an *event*, which some things are capable of causing in some human beings. On the other hand, beauty, like poisonousness, is not an event or a quality, but a *capacity*—the capacity some things have of causing pleasure in *some* contemplative beholders of them. This capacity, however, is *manifest*—that is, beauty is experienced—only at the times when one of these beholders contemplates an object that has it; just as the poisonousness of arsenic is manifest instead of latent only when it is poisoning somebody, or the combustibility of paper is manifest only when it is burning.

What Makes a Pleasure Aesthetic

To the account of the nature of beauty just given, three objections may suggest themselves that are plausible at first sight and with which we must now deal. The first is that, although indeed the beautiful is pleasure-giving, many pleasure-giving things are not beautiful—that is, pleasure, is not always aesthetic pleasure. Thus, it still remains for us to say what differentiates aesthetic pleasure from pleasure of other sorts and beautiful things from pleasure-giving things that are not beautiful.

The needed differentiating character, however, actually appears in the definition of "the beautiful" given above, but its differentiating power easily escapes notice unless pointed out. The definition, it should be noticed, does not characterize the beautiful object simply as one that can cause pleasure in us, but as one that can do so in the mere aesthetic contemplation of it. The nature of aesthetic contemplation has already been described, and it is by reference to it that aesthetic pleasures are distinguished from other pleasures. What makes a pleasure aesthetic is not some pecularity intrinsic to it, but only the fact that the pleasure is one being obtained through the mere contemplation of the object that is the source of it. That is, in order that an object be found beautiful, it is necessary that the relation of it to us, in which it causes pleasure in us, be the particular one consisting of aesthetic contemplation of the object by us.

No One's Taste Demonstrably Good or Bad

The second of the objections alluded to above is based on the existence of so-called canons, or rules, of beauty—unity, rhythm, balance, and so on. These, it is pointed out, are objective characters, not subjective and variable reactions, like pleasure. And it is then argued that if beauty is determined by them, it too is then objective.

In answer to this, however, it may be pointed out, first, that even if the argument were logically sound—which, as we shall see, it is not—it would apply only to beauty of form and not to beauty of material or to what Santayana calls "beauty of expression." This classification of the possible sources of the beauty of a beautiful object not only has bearing, as just suggested, on the contention we are examining, but is of fundamental importance for aesthetics. We may therefore well take this occasion to say what is needed to make clear the meaning of that classification.

The word "form," in connection with art, has been used variously and often with only vague meaning. When, however, aesthetic form is contrasted with aesthetic material, form means essentially *arrangement* and material means *whatever it is that is arranged*. A line, for example, is an arrangement of points; and a square or a triangle is an arrangement of straight lines. A patch of color, again, is an arrangement of colored points, but two-dimensional; whereas a straight line is a one-dimensional arrangement. A melody, similarly, is an arrangement of tones; a dance, an arrangement of movements; and so on.

That form is one possible source of beauty and material another may be shown by a simple experiment. A square of gray, for example, and one of violet have the same form; in both cases the shape is the same, and the color has the same unity. Yet most persons would judge one more beautiful than the other. The difference in beauty not being due in this instance to difference of form has to be ascribed to the difference of material—that is, of color. On the other hand, if two patches are of exactly the same color but of different shapes, and one is judged more pleasing aesthetically than the other, this can only be due to the difference of form.

But in addition to form and material, there is another possible source of beauty in an object, namely, the associations the object happens to have had in the mind of the beholder. As Santayana has pointed out, if these associations have been pleasant ones, and if perception of the object stirs them without calling them explicitly to mind, then the pleasantness that really belongs to them is for us, as it were, borrowed from them by the object and is felt by us as possessed by the object itself. The object, that is to say, acquires through these associations the capacity to cause pleasure in us in the mere act of contemplation, which means that it is insofar beautiful for us.

Beauty traceable to this source is often called beauty of expression, but "expression" is then being

used in the sense of "meaning" or "connotation";
and since "expression" in aesthetics is used also,
indeed in most instances, to refer to the activity of
the artist when he is creating an object embodying
his intent, the misunderstandings that, because of
this, often result from the term "beauty of expression"
would be avoided if another term were used instead.
"Beauty of connotation" would seem to be the one
most clearly descriptive of what is meant; or, better
still, "beauty through connotation," for of course it is
the object itself, not its connotation, that has the
beauty. The associations that constitute the connotation through which the object becomes beautiful
need not themselves be beautiful; they need to be
pleasant; but not necessarily *aesthetically* pleasant.

These explanations will have made clear what was
meant earlier when, to the remark that the so-called
canons of beauty are formulated in terms of objective
characters, it was replied that these canons, in any
case, have to do, not with all beauty, but only with
beauty of form. But now we may go on to point out
that, even as regards beauty of form, universal agreement—if it were a fact—as to the objective characters
(such as unity, rhythm, balance, and so forth) on
which this beauty depends would, of course, not show
that it is not also dependent on the contemplative
beholder's pleasure. For to say that the canons of
beauty formulated in terms of these characters have
universal validity could mean simply that these characters happen to give pleasure to *all* such beholders.

And that it would mean just this is suggested by the reflection that, if *nobody* found objects conforming to those canons pleasant to contemplate, it would then be hard to think of any reason for still calling such objects beautiful.

The fact is, however, that not *everybody's* aesthetic pleasure is dependent on conformity of the object to those canons. For there are some persons, even if perhaps not many, who are not pleased but bored by things that obey these so-called canons of beauty; and who, on the contrary, enjoy things that patently violate them. One may, of course, call their taste anarchistic, jazzy, or perverse, but this does not do away with the fact that such persons exist; nor does it prove their taste bad, unless one arbitrarily defines as "good" the taste of those who find beautiful the things that instead conform to those alleged rules.

Those rules, thus, are not in any sense standards to which a person's taste "ought" to conform, even when it actually does not; they are merely statements of certain formal characteristics upon which depends the aesthetic pleasure of whom? Of none other than those persons whose aesthetic pleasure happens to depend upon them! That these persons are in the majority is probably true, but this in no way condemns the taste of the minority whose canons of beauty are different from those. Beauty, being in the manner already described a matter of the pleasure caused in the contemplative observer, is as variable and as relative to the individual's nature as is pleasure itself.

How Perfection Inheres in Beauty

The third of the objections to which reference was made is more significant than the two that have now been considered, since it points to a need, not indeed to take back anything we have so far said about the nature of beauty, but to make a certain important addition to it. The objection is that the notion of beauty somehow implies that of perfection or near perfection of the object found beautiful—of a certain approach by it to an ideal—and that the definition of beauty we have given ignores this. A consequence is that, according to our definition, the pretty, the charming, the graceful—since they give pleasure in contemplation—would be instances of the beautiful; whereas, in fact, they often are much rather contrasted with it. Thus one frequently hears it said of some girl, for instance, that she is pretty though not beautiful; or of some woman that she is no beauty, but is graceful or charming.

There is no doubt that this use of the adjective "beautiful" is the ordinary one. On the other hand, as A. C. Bradley points out in his *Oxford Lectures on Poetry,* only aestheticians use the adjective to designate whatever has positive aesthetic value, irrespective of whether this value be of the sort more specifically called prettiness, or charm, or beauty in the ordinary narrower sense, or sublimity, or grace, and so on. We do need a term that will be inclusive of all these, but it is unfortunate that aestheticians should have picked the term "beautiful"; for this term has long been in common use in the narrower sense that excludes these other categories of positive aesthetic value. The confusion that has resulted from this in discussions of beauty has been the greater because aestheticians have often not realized that, when they spoke of beauty and attempted to analyze its nature, they were speaking of and analyzing something not the same as what the term ordinarily refers to.

The analysis of beauty previously given concerned beauty in that inclusive or generic sense. It provided a statement of what is meant by "possession of positive aesthetic value," no matter of which specific sort, by an object. But just because it concerned beauty generically, what it said is true also—but is not the whole truth—about beauty in the ordinary narrower sense, which excludes the other species of positive aesthetic value. Accordingly, what now remains to be pointed out is what the adjective "beautiful" means —in addition to "capable of causing pleasure in the mere contemplation"—when, in ordinary language, a horse or a flower, for example, is called beautiful.

"Beautiful" in such cases means that the given object not only is pleasing to contemplate, but is as much or nearly as much so as the *most* pleasing thing of its kind that we are at the time able to imagine. Just this is the manner in which the idea of perfection enters into ordinary judgments of beauty. It is quite true that they are made in the light of an ideal, of an image of a perfect thing. This ideal, however, is always one relevant *only to the particular kind to which the given object belongs.* That is, if the object is a horse, its beauty is judged by reference to the ideal or perfect horse, not to the ideal cow or tree or mountain.

Moreover, the sort of perfection concerned is essentially aesthetic perfection, not instrumental or biological or other perfection, except insofar as these other types of perfection might happen to contribute to aesthetic perfection. This would require that the other sort of perfection be both evident and itself causative of pleasure in contemplation. Thus, to be one's aesthetic ideal—one's image of perfection—for objects of a given kind, means to be the most pleasing object of that kind to contemplate that one is able to imagine.

These remarks make clear that there are indeed standards or ideals of beauty—one for each kind of thing—in the light of which we make our judgments of beauty. But these standards, let it be well noted, are both personal and likely to change; for the nature of the most pleasing thing of a given kind to contemplate that a given person is at a given time able to imagine largely depends on how extensive and diversified has been his experience with things of that kind. The imagination has the power to pick and choose, and to combine into one whole various pleasing characters that one or another of the objects previously experienced exhibited, but that were never found together in one object. The imagination, indeed, can go even farther, and invent and add to the imaginary picture pleasing characters one never yet

has met with. But it can do this only to a limited extent and, in constructing its ideals, has to depend
mainly on the felicitous traits it has previously
found here and there. As new examples of objects of
the given kind enter the individual's experience,
some of them are likely to display pleasing characters
he had not before found or imagined, but that he
will now incorporate into his mental picture of the
ideal for the kind of thing concerned. This means
that his standards of beauty gradually evolve.

The chief among the puzzles with which the facts
about beauty confront us having now, it may be
hoped, been resolved, let us turn to those that attend
the criticism of art.

CHAPTER V

THE CRITICISM OF ART

CRITICS of the various arts, and especially critics of literature, not only discuss given works of the particular art in which they are interested, but also occasionally write essays on criticism. In these, they generally state and argue for the opinion they personally hold as to what criticism ought to be. That is, they mention certain types of questions that a critic ought to answer concerning the books, paintings, musical compositions, or theatrical performances that he discusses; and they also often mention certain other questions that they hold to be irrelevant, and therefore not to be asked by any critic who really knows his business.

But the task of the aesthetician, insofar as it concerns criticism, is different from that which such essays undertake. The aesthetician does not attempt to say what the criticism of literature, painting, or any other art ought to be; and he therefore does not take sides in the controversies between individual critics or between rival schools of criticism. He attempts to say, not what criticism ought to be, but what essentially it is, no matter by what school represented or upon which art directed. The aesthetician, that is to say, claims no God-given or other authority to prescribe norms or standards of criticism. He only attempts to describe what any such norms or standards consist in, what varieties of them there are, and the limits of relevance of each. He attempts to view the whole enterprise of criticism from above—objectively, impartially, and in the perspective of the variety of human interests.

This, it will perhaps be said, is a beautiful program, but one that seems to partake too much of the grandiloquent vagueness that always has been the besetting sin of philosophy. Yet, that the program is not really as vague as it may sound will, I believe, become evident if we turn to the specific questions that it is the business of the philosophy of art criticism to answer. The first of these is whether it is not perhaps true that the word "criticism" is used, often unawares, in at least two very different senses; so that not one kind of enterprise only, but in fact two or even more are given this same name, notwithstanding that they are wholly or largely independent of one another.

The verb "to criticize" is commonly used mostly in the sense of "to find fault with," "to pass adverse judgment on." Yet, that the judgment passed is adverse is not an implication of the etymology of the verb, since the Greek κρίνειν (*krinein*) means simply to discern or to judge. More closely in accordance with the derivation of the verb, therefore, is the also current and somewhat more technical use of "to criticize" in the sense of "to pass judgment, whether favorable or unfavorable," "to judge of the merits or demerits of something," "to evaluate."

But further, judgment is not necessarily judgment of worth. Not only evaluation but also mere description involves the exercise of judgment; and thus the word "criticism" is, without impropriety, often used also to designate simply the scientific investigation and description of the text, origins, character, structure, technique, history or historical context, and so on, of a work of literature or of one of the other arts. When the word "criticism" is used in this sense, a critic is then a person whose knowledge, training, and interests presumably equip him to study and describe a given work *critically*—that is, with discernment as to such matters as just mentioned.

Unfortunately, it seems often not to be realized that criticism in this sense is not automatically also criticism in the sense of judgment of worth; that it is essentially description, not appraisal; that it involves scholarly research and painstaking observation, but does not necessarily involve either the exercise of taste or evaluation on some other basis. Indeed, if a person engaged in scholarly investigation of the authorship, text, history, or technique of a given work happened to be also a person having pronounced tastes of his own as regards works of the field concerned, the objectivity of his judgments concerning these matters might easily be impaired. Therefore it has been said by an eminent writer on the subject that to be a good critic a man should have no taste!

There is, of course, no reason why a man who makes a critical study of the text or of the historical context of a given work should not also judge its merits; but it must be emphasized that although both activities alike are called criticism, each is criticism in a different sense. Indeed, just as criticism in the sense of scholarly study is possible without criticism in the sense of appraisal, so is appraisal sometimes possible without scholarly study. One may very well be able to say that, in certain respects, a given work is good or bad, without knowing anything about its date, its author, history, or technique.

This statement, doubtless will be shocking to many and will probably arouse vigorous denial. I shall soon consider the grounds on which the denial would ordinarily be based; but in the meantime the assertion may be supported by the fact that, in order to judge as good or bad the aroma of a cigar or the bouquet of a wine, one need not know where the tobacco or the grapes were grown, nor how the tobacco was cured or the wine made, nor how old the latter is. Or again, if one is served at dinner an unfamiliar dish, one can very well judge whether its taste is good or bad, or better than that of some other, without knowing what the ingredients are, where they come from, or how they were cooked. Perhaps it will be objected that judgments of taste as to wines, cigars, or food are radically different from judgments of taste as to music, painting, or literature. But although this opinion is widespread, I believe it to be a profound error. At all events, readiness to make the claim is far more often met than is readiness to show in what the alleged fundamental difference consists.

Criticism as Investigation of Text, Context, or Technique

Let us now turn to some of the things undertaken by criticism conceived as scholarly investigation, and let us inquire how far or whether at all investigation of them is, as often alleged, prerequisite or ancillary to criticism conceived as judgment of worth.

There is first what, in the case of a work of literature, is called textual criticism—namely, the scientific attempt to establish the original form of the work; or, in the case of a book, such as the *Bible,* also perhaps the attempt to determine the portions of a given part traceable to some author or authors other than the one to whom that part is traditionally ascribed.

Evidently, the question how important or unimportant textual criticism is for purposes of literary or ethical or other appraisal depends on what exactly it is that we intend to appraise. If, for instance, it is the book now on my table—which happens to be a copy of the King James version of the *Bible*—then I submit that its literary style, or the soundness of its ethical or religious precepts, and a number of other things about it can be appraised wholly without reference to such questions as to whether it is an accurate translation, or whether the text from which it was translated was itself corrupt, or who were its authors, and so on. The literary, ethical, and other merits that

countless persons have found the King James *Bible*
to possess have been merits that its text had for them
as it stood.

But if what we are interested in appraising were
instead *God's* literary style or the worth of his precepts, then it would be important indeed that we
should know as exactly as possible what originally he
dictated to the scribes whom he inspired to take the
pen.

The text we are interested in appraising may be
difficult to establish; or it may be one already at
hand, no matter how it came to be as it is. But in
either case historical information of one kind or another has importance for the appreciation or evalu-
tion of a literary work only to the extent that such
information is needed to enable us to understand
the statements we read in it—to the extent, for example, needed to understand allusions made in it; or
to explain the meaning of words in it no longer in
use; or to explain the nature of the customs and be-
liefs of the place and time the book is about, on
which perhaps turns the dramatic character of some
situation it depicts; and so on. But investigation of
such historical matters easily and often becomes so
engrossing to those who carry it on that appreciation
or evaluation of the work itself, although it is the end
to which the historical study was originally intended
to be a means, is soon forgotten. And the historical
investigation, being pursued then wholly for the interest found in the pursuit itself, is accordingly carried into details or directions that no longer have any

shadow of relevance to judgment of the merits of the given work.

To point this out is not at all to disparage such minute historical studies. They are genuine manifestations of the true scientific spirit—of the pure love of knowledge—which is as admirable here as in mathematics or palaeontology; and they are self-justifying to the persons who carry them on and to others similarly curious about the facts concerned. I wish only to stress that the justification of these minute studies lies in the intrinsic interest they have for *these* persons, and not, contrary to what is often claimed, in any need of them for purposes of enjoyment or evaluation of the works concerned. By the scholars devoted to such studies, works of literature or of the other arts are really being viewed much as a professional anatomist may be conceived to view his friends—as splendid specimens for eventual dissection!

In the case of a painting, the analogue of textual criticism would consist of inquiry into what the painting was originally like; who really painted it; what alterations, if any, were subsequently made in it and by whom; and so on. A person expert in the investigation of such matters is a specialized detective and is insofar a critic only in the sense in which a detective on the police force, who knows the "styles," fingerprints, and favorite materials of various local burglars, may be called a critic of burglaries. Like the latter, a person who is a critic of paintings in this sense makes use of all the resources of the laboratory:

X-rays, chemical analysis of pigments, microscopic study of fibers of the canvas, illumination by light of selected wave lengths, and even fingerprints if a painter happens to have left any in the paint of his pictures.

But here too the importance or unimportance of all this for purposes of aesthetic appreciation and appraisal depends on whether what we are essentially concerned to appreciate or evaluate is this painting itself as it now stands before us or, let us say, paintings by a given seventeenth-century painter. In the latter case, presumably, we would lose interest in the painting before us if the fact were established that it had been painted by someone else; whereas in the former, the authorship and history of the painting are as irrelevant to our purpose as is knowledge of the name of the cook or of the recipe to our enjoyment or appraisal of the savor of a particular dish. Nothing but a sensitive tongue is needed for this; and, similarly as regards the painting, what is needed and all that is needed, is sensitivity to subtle differences in such things as colors, lines, shapes, values, arrangement, and expression.

This kind of sensitivity may be present in persons who know little or nothing of the history or the technique of painting; and it may well be absent in persons who, on the contrary, have a vast store of knowledge of this kind. Thus, to be capable of aesthetic appreciation of a painting is one thing; to be able to discuss its history, its technique, or the traditions that influenced the painter, quite another. Neither capacity necessarily entails or requires the other.

The courses given in museums, colleges and universities, or other schools in what is called the appreciation of painting, music, literature, or the other arts generally are offered and taken, at least in part, under the assumption that knowledge of the history, and forms, and techniques of a given art automatically enhances sensitivity to the aesthetic values of the works of this art. But this assumption is, I believe, in large part an error. What does beget increased aesthetic sensitivity is firsthand acquaintance with a wide variety of the works of the given art, together with absorbed and repeated contemplation of them and comparison of them directly with one another. Insofar as this diversified, intense, and comparative *direct* aesthetic experience is made a part of a course in appreciation, the course will indeed tend to develop the capacity for aesthetic response in those who take the course. But the point I wish to emphasize is that, for this purpose, lectures, readings, and discussions of the history, technique, and forms of a given art never are a possible substitute for abundant firsthand experience of the kind described.

This, I take it, will generally be admitted; but it is widely believed that the historical and technical information to be gained from lectures and reading also greatly contributes to the enhancement of aesthetic appreciation. Yet I believe that the effect of systematic study of such matters is much rather to inhibit the aesthetic interest in works of art, and to make habitual instead the intellectual, inquisitive, scholarly interest. The search for knowledge concerning the history, the human context and social import, or the technique of given works of art is, of course, a perfectly legitimate pursuit; and I would be the last to disparage or overlook the values of knowledge, since they are the very ones for which I, like other philosophers, mostly live. I insist only that knowledge—even knowlege about art—although it is as noble and fine as aesthetic response, is nevertheless a different sort of thing; that enjoyment of it is intellectual, not aesthetic, enjoyment; and that the discipline which fits one for intellectual enjoyment not only does not automatically develop one's capacity for aesthetic appreciation, but rather tends to inhibit and displace it.

Knowledge of the technique of an art doubtless does much for the person who possesses it, but it also does something *to* him. The actor in the audience at a play perceives mostly the acting, not the play; the story writer who reads a story is conscious less of the story told than of the literary devices by which interest is aroused, suspense induced, or an end made after the climax; the painter who looks at another painter's picture sees, not a picture, but only or mainly such things as edges, the colors of shadows, the scale of values, brushing technique, composition, proportions, the handling of corners, and so forth. And what historical knowledge about art does to its possessor is shown by the fact that, for the scholar, a

story by Flaubert or a picture by Van Gogh is mainly
an occasion for an hour's discourse on the life of the
artist, or his psychological make-up, or the influence
of others upon his art and of himself upon others, or
the date and history of the particular work considered, or the features typical of the author's style.
What the training of a critic in this sense of the word
does is to fit him to talk and talk and talk, learnedly
and esoterically, about works of the particular art he
has studied; but it does not automatically enhance his
capacity for appreciation or evaluation of their aesthetic merits or defects.

This, I believe, is not sufficiently realized. An
archaeologist, for instance, easily comes to regard
himself and to be regarded by others as an authority,
not only on the history, but also on the aesthetic
merits of the statues or other objects he digs up. Yet
he may, in fact, be less capable of aesthetic response
to them than was perhaps one of the laborers hired by
him to do the digging. This possibility is masked by
the fact already pointed out that the name "criticism" is applied both to scholarly investigation of a
work of art and to appraisal of its merits. Moreover,
because scholarly study of works of art is capable of
being gratifyingly scientific, and is therefore capable
of reaching demonstrably objective conclusions, the
temptation is strong to believe that such study is
what criticism *really* is or should be, and that criticism in any other sense is unimportant because subjective. The truth, however, is that criticism in the
sense of judgment of value is neither less nor more

important than criticism in the sense of historical study, but is the manifestation simply of an interest of quite a different kind in the same object.

Merit Not Implied by Conformity to Type

There is, however, an objection to what I have been maintaining, which is plausible at first sight and will doubtless already have suggested itself. It is that, after all, there are in each art certain traditional art forms, as in poetry the sonnet or in music the sonata; and that it is not possible to judge whether a poem is a good sonnet or a musical composition a good sonata unless one knows just what formal characters differentiate the sonnet or the sonata from other poetical or musical forms.

It is quite true, of course, that one must know this; but to suppose that the contentions I have set forth are thereby invalidated is to overlook the difference between good and good of a kind. That some things which are good or even perfect instances of their kind may nevertheless be bad things is sufficiently shown by the example mentioned by the late Professor G. H. Palmer, of the little boy who was crying because, as he said, he had just had a *good* spanking. Obviously, the better a spanking, the worse it is to receive. Or again, there is such a thing as a good burglary or a perfect forgery, or indeed a perfect devil as well as a perfect angel. In such instances, the adjectives "good" and "perfect" are not essentially adjectives of value, but only signify possession in a high degree, or in the highest degree, of the characteristics distinctive of the kind of thing considered. And the kind may be bad. Thus forgery is bad, and a good forgery is worse than a bad forgery.

It is true that we may admire the skill even of a forgery, to say nothing of that exhibited in a painting or a poem; but we must not confuse evaluation of the virtuosity of the creator of an object with evaluation of the object itself. An admirably done thing is not necessarily an admirable thing. Admiration of an object because of the skill that was needed to create it is essentially admiration of a stunt; and appreciation of its difficulty and of the performer's success in overcoming that difficulty is no more aesthetic appreciation in the case of a musical or pictorial or poetical stunt than it is in the case of the feats of a strong man, a sword swallower, or a contortionist. Admiration can be excited by many things other than beauty.

Moreover, it is well to remember that, at least in the visual arts, where genres and art forms are not so stereotyped as, for example, in music or poetry, the judgments we make ascribing to skill this or that feature of the work before us are highly subjective and precarious. The fact that a certain feature of the object pleases us does not necessarily signify that it was something the artist intended and had the skill to achieve. It may well be the effect, not of skill, but of accident; or even of what the artist himself regards as a mistake or blunder that he was not quite skillful enough to correct.

But, to give the objection on which I have been

commenting as much force as it can have, let us consider its effect in the sort of example most favorable
to it. Let us assume that the kind defined by given requirements as to form happens to be a pleasing kind.
This for many persons would be true, for instance, of
the kind of poem called the sonnet. The question
then is whether, in order to decide whether a given
instance of that good kind is a good instance of it,
we need to know what characteristics differentiate
the sonnet from other poetical forms.

The answer is that we do need to know this, but do
not need to know it discursively. That is, we need to
be able in practice to recognize a given poem as being
a sonnet if it happens to be one, but we do not need
to know, analytically, the list of defining characters
that differentiate a sonnet from poems of all other
types. If we can recognize a poem as a sonnet and
have read a good many other sonnets in the past, we
have what we need in order to evaluate it as a good
or bad sonnet, or as better or worse than another.

The situation is substantially the same as in the
case of a rose. To be in position to judge whether a
given flower is a good, fair, or poor example of the
kind called the rose, we do not need to be able to list
the differentiating characters of the rose. If we are
able to recognize a rose when we see one and have
seen a good many roses, we have all we need to judge
the aesthetic merits of a given rose as compared with
other roses. It is only when the goodness or badness
of an instance of a given kind is defined in terms of
certain arbitrarily selected points—as, for example,

are the "merits" of Mexican hairless dogs at a dog show—that knowledge of a list of those points is necessary. Judgment on such a basis, however, is virtually again judgment of a stunt—a stunt performed in the case of the dog by nature or by a breeder.

Criticism as Appraisal

What has been said up to this point will, I assume, have been sufficient to make clear that the word "criticism" is equivocal—sometimes meaning scholarly discussion of historical or textual matters, or of matters of technique; and sometimes, on the other hand, meaning judgment as to the merits of given works. Let us now pass to criticism in this latter, more common, sense.

It might seem, as regards the merits of a given work, that there would be little more to say than that it is good or bad, or better or worse than certain others. A certain *prima facie* plausibility is given to this opinion by the fact that the number of adjectives —such as good, bad, beautiful, ugly, sublime, noble, and so on—that are adjectives specifically of *value* is very small as compared with the number of adjectives, ordinarily contrasted with them as simply *descriptive,* that signify characters other than values.

But when we turn to what is actually said about given works of art by persons who are critics in the sense that they judge the values, positive or negative, of those works, we find that value adjectives, such as just mentioned, are rather seldom used by them.

How it is that their judgments are nevertheless judgments of value is, at first, something of a puzzle. But
the puzzle is solved as soon as we notice that the very
same statement can at one time be used to express a
merely descriptive and purely objective judgment,
and at another time to express in addition a judgment of value. Whether the statement does express a
judgment of value or not on a given occasion depends on whether a certain assumption is or is not
then being made. The statement that a given work
possesses a certain objective characteristic expresses
at the same time a judgment of value if the characteristic is one that the judging person approves or,
as the case may be, disapproves; and is thus one that
he regards as conferring, respectively, positive or
negative value on any object of the given kind that
happens to possess it. But if, on the contrary, the assumption that the given characteristic is a valued or
disvalued one is not made, then the statement that
the object has this characteristic is not evaluative but
descriptive only.

For example, the statement that a given novel runs
to half-a-million words is descriptive of a certain perfectly objective and verifiable character of it, and
may be intended as purely descriptive. But it may be
intended to express, in addition, an adverse comment
on the given novel, under the tacit assumption that
it is a *bad* thing in any novel to be as long as that.
Again, the statement that the style of a certain author
is repetitious may be intended as purely descriptive;

but ordinarily it would be intended to convey, and would convey in addition, the judgment that, because of this, his style is tedious and therefore bad.

It should be noticed also that the very same adjective may express favorable evaluation when applied to things of a certain sort, but unfavorable when applied to things of certain other sorts. The adjective "involved," for instance, as applied to the plot of a mystery story, is a term of praise; but when applied to a piece of reasoning, it is a term of blame.

Evaluative criticism, thus, actually consists not so much in saying simply that a given work is good or bad, or better or worse than another, as in saying in effect that it is so in consequence of its possessing this or that specific feature, which the critic regards as a good or a bad one for a work of that kind to possess. The sorts of features that a given critic approves or disapproves of, for works of a given kind, constitute the *standards of criticism* which he uses for evaluation of works of that kind.

The great difference between the judgments of goodness and badness passed by a trained critic and those passed by the ordinary, unsophisticated consumer of art is that the critic traces his evaluation of the object he is judging to the specific features that make it for him predominantly pleasing or displeasing; whereas the unsophisticated amateur of art is pleased or displeased by the given object without knowing which, in particular, are the features that cause the pleasure or displeasure he finds in it. *That*

*is, the ordinary amateur's judgment of value is whole-
sale, unanalytical; that of the critic, detailed, analytical.*

But the true amateur, who is not a mere echo,
nevertheless has a taste of his own and knows
whether it is being gratified or offended. This is true
also of the critic; but the critic knows in addition,
and is able to describe, what specific sorts of characters do gratify or offend his taste.

It is very important here, however, to guard
against a certain widespread illusion concerning the
critic's judgment, namely, the illusion that mention
by him of the specific grounds of his approval or dis-
approval of a given work constitutes proof or evidence that his judgment of its value is true or right,
and is authoritative over that of a person who is not
similarly able to give the grounds of his likes and dislikes—so that the latter person is held not really qualified to judge; and if his judgment differs from that of
the critic, it is held to be wrong and his taste bad.
This is an opinion very common indeed not only, as
one might expect, among critics, but also among ordinary amateurs of art, who in general are deplorably
humble and easily awed. But it is nevertheless an
error.

This becomes evident as soon as we notice what
happens if the critic is challenged to say, not why he
likes a given painting, for example, but why he likes
those specific features of the painting that he gives as
the basis for his approval. To make the matter concrete, let us suppose that, when asked why he judges

a certain painting good, the critic answers that, for one thing, it is because the plastic qualities of the objects in it are adequately represented. Then, when asked further why this characteristic is a good one in a painting, he may reply that it is a characteristic distinctive of all painting that is genuinely art. But obviously this reply merely begs the question. It is an implict and probably unconscious, but nevertheless arbitrary, proposal by him to set up as a standard of what is genuine art in painting that which he personally values so highly; and to label as irrelevant that, for instance, which he would call the narrative and sentimental aspects of the painting. But, of course, question-begging epithets prove nothing on either side.

The long and short of the situation is thus that the critic is personally much interested in plastic qualities and not interested, or less interested, in the other things that a painter may also or instead be interested in and be attempting to express. Accordingly, when our critic is challenged to justify his own high valuation of plastic qualities, there is in the end nothing he can say, except that they interest and delight *him*.

This, of course, is a sufficient answer so far as he personally is concerned; but the English couple whom William James overheard in the Academy in Venice sentimentalizing over the expression of abnegation on the Virgin's face in Titian's "Assumption" had exactly the same sort of justification for their valuing the picture because of that expression,

rather than because of its plastic qualities. James, it is
true, characterizes their sentiment as spurious and as
something that "would have fairly made old Titian
sick." But, after all, Titian did put on the Virgin's
face an expression of abnegation and not, for instance, a sneer, as he could just as easily have done.
He put it there, presumably, because he *intended* her
face to express abnegation; and one may therefore
doubt whether he would, as James alleges, have been
made sick by the fact that these people were getting
out of his painting something he had chosen to put
into it. I venture he might rather have been mildly
amused at their blindness to the *other* things he had
put there also.

The critic's evaluations, then, ultimately are just
as purely matters of his individual taste as are those
of the unsophisticated amateur. The great difference,
even when both of them have the same tastes, is, as
already pointed out, that the naïve amateur is
pleased or displeased without knowing exactly why,
whereas the critic does know what specific features
are responsible for his own pleasure or displeasure
in a given work of art. But in both cases the situation
is in the end just the same as with, let us say, the taste
of pineapple. Some persons like it, and others dislike
it; but it would be absurd to say that it is *really* good,
although some dislike it, or *really* bad, although some
like it. For when the values concerned are not instrumental values but immediate values—whether of
odors, of tastes, of sounds, of plastic qualities, or of

facial expressions—then individual likes and dislikes constitute the only meaning of good and bad.

A person's tastes, thus—whether he be sophisti-cated critic or simple amateur—are ultimately at once incapable of justification and self-justifying. And therefore, in the matter of tastes, there can be no dis-puting but, as Oscar Wilde pointed out, only quarrel-ling. We can indeed apply epithets to persons whose taste differs from ours; we can despise them, howl them down, and ostracize them. But we cannot possi-bly prove that their taste is bad in any sense other than that it is *different* from ours, or different from that of a majority or of some other particular group to which we ourselves belong or would like to belong. There is no such thing as *objective* goodness or bad-ness of taste, but only such a thing as my taste and your taste, the taste of this man and the taste of some other man, tastes shared by many or by few.

A person's taste may change, of course, but whether we call the change development or perversion de-pends solely on whether it changes in the direction of our own or away from it. A change in our own taste is for each of us, by definition, development—not perversion.

A person's taste, again, may be indeed more *sensi-tive* than that of another, in the objective sense that he is able to get pleasure or displeasure from differ-ences in the object that, to the other person, make no difference. But the latter will then call the other "oversophisticated," "effete," "precious," "morbidly sensitive," and so on; and the former will, in retort, fling at him such epithets as "crude," "coarse," "undiscerning," and the like. That is, the question whether greater sensitiveness of taste than a given person possesses is itself a good or a bad thing is decided or decidable by us on no other ground than whether we ourselves have it or would like to have it, or whether we do not have it or harbor contempt for it.

That there is no such thing as goodness or badness of taste in an objective, universally valid sense is a fact that profoundly disturbs some persons when they first come up against it. It seems to them to make art criticism impossible. But so to conclude is to mistake the import of the fact. As pointed out above, art criticism in aesthetic terms actually consists in analysis, by the critic, of the features of a given work of art that determine his liking or disliking it. That his evaluation of these features themselves is a matter of his own taste or interests leaves criticism in that sense perfectly possible. What is taken away is only the illusion that such criticism proves something and is authoritative over the evaluations of less analytical persons. To lose this illusion, however, does not entail that one no longer has a taste of one's own. Rather, the realization that there are no authorities in matters of taste throws one back upon one's own taste, frees one from distrust of it, and enlivens it. But realization of this also gives one a sense of humor about one's taste. That is, it replaces, by a certain abstract tolerance, the sneers or even sometimes the

fury that before would almost have denied the right
to exist to persons whose taste shockingly diverged
from ours.

Appraisal in Terms Other Than Aesthetic

What has been said so far concerns the evaluation
of works of art in terms of beauty and ugliness—that
is, in terms of the pleasure or displeasure caused by
a work in a beholder who contemplates it aesthetically. But it must now be emphasized that evaluation of a work of art thus in aesthetic terms is far
from being the only possible or legitimate type of
evaluation. Indeed, aesthetic evaluation does not
even have priority over other types of evaluation, except in the case of persons whose own interest in the
given work is predominantly aesthetic. Evaluation of
a painting or of a book in terms of, for instance, religious values, is possible and quite as legitimate;
and, for persons interested primarily in such values,
is more relevant. The example of Tolstoi comes to
mind in this connection. This important fact will
become more evident if mention is now made of
some of the principal terms, other than aesthetic, in
which works of art may be evaluated.

There is first of all the consideration in terms of
which the artist himself, at each moment as he creates the work, evaluates and, if need be, corrects
what he has done. This consideration might be, but
except in works of decorative art usually is not,
whether what he has done is beautiful or ugly.

Rather, what he asks himself is whether what he has done does or does not adequately express what he is attempting to express. As already pointed out, beauty bears to the work of the artist the same sort of relation that truth does to the statement any one of us makes of a given idea that comes to him. Doubtless, in most cases we hope the idea is true; but if to say something true had been our essential concern, then any other true statement—as, for instance, that July follows June, would have done just as well. Our essential concern, rather, is to express adequately the specific idea we have at the time; and it is in terms of adequacy or inadequacy to this objective that our statement is evaluated by us and, if need be, corrected. The same is true of the emotional intuitions the artist is attempting to express on a given occasion. If what at the time he feels moved to paint is, let us say, a human figure, then the painting of a landscape, even if equally or more beautiful, is not a possible substitute.

Another consideration in the light of which the artist may criticize a finished work of his own is whether what it expresses is something that, on reflection, he is willing to acknowledge as a part of himself. Our own moods, feelings, attitudes, and sentiments, like our own thoughts, are made clear to us if we succeed in expressing them objectively. The object created—whether it be a painting, a melody, or a sentence—is a mirror that reflects back to us the feeling or the thought we had within us, and allows us to scrutinize and evaluate it more carefully than we could before. And it may well be that we then disapprove of that aspect of ourself which the mirror exhibits to us. In such a case, we may reject the work we have created, not because it expresses inadequately what we had to express, but because what it does adequately express is something that indeed was, but is no longer, a part of ourself. We have transcended, and now disown, the feeling the work objectifies.

Again, a work of art may be evaluated, as Tolstoi proposed, in terms of its adequacy as an instrument for the transmission to other persons of the emotional experience its creator had to express. For it is conceivable that the work might express the artist's insight adequately, but in a code language, as it were, which other persons understand perhaps imperfectly or not at all. Adequacy of the work *qua* instrument for the communication to others of what the artist felt is a sort of merit that the artist himself, as a gregarious being, may desire; and is also something that a spectator may legitimately demand if what he is interested in is sharing the artist's emotional experience. Only rough tests of such adequacy are possible, however, since there is no way of comparing directly the feeling the artist seeks to express with the feeling the spectator obtains.

On the other hand, the spectator has a perfect right to evaluate, if he wishes, a work of art simply in terms of its emotional import to himself or to beholders in general, irrespective of whether this import is or is not the import the artist intended his work to have.

Indeed, *when a work of art is considered from the point of view of the consumer, the values in terms of which it may legitimately be appraised by him are of the most diverse sorts.* They may be aesthetic values; but they may equally well be moral, political, or even commercial value. Or, appraisal may be in terms of the educational value of the given work— in terms, that is to say, of its capacity to initiate the consumer into sentiments, attitudes, or moods hitherto unexperienced by him. Literature especially is susceptible of being evaluated by most varied standards, since often it is a "mixed" art, in the sense that it aims to express not only feelings for their own sakes but also certain ideas. That is, these ideas are then not mere means used by the writer to the end of expressing certain feelings arousable only through ideas, but are ideas that he regards as objectively important and wishes to disseminate.

A book, accordingly, may be appraised in terms of its informativeness or in terms of its effectiveness as propaganda for a cause in which the reader is interested. Another book may be prized by some because it furnishes an agreeable escape from so-called reality, and yet condemned by others for the very same reason. Some will value a book on account of its vivid depiction of a certain stratum of society; others will be primarily concerned with beauty, or quaintness,

or originality of style; others perhaps with philosophical profundity; and so on.

Of these various terms in which it is possible to
appraise a book or some other work of art, none
can be claimed to be *the* objectively right terms.
Prospectors have a saying that "gold is where you
find it"; and we may say conversely that a given book
or other work of art is genuinely a mine of whatever
species of value somebody does, in fact, find in it.
The claim that one *ought* to seek this or that particular sort of value in a given work is sheer dogmatism;
it is but an instinctive attempt to make one's own
angle of interest obligatory for everybody.

The Services Critics Can Render

Against this background let us now ask what function, if any, does the professional art critic have in
society. The function he is most generally supposed
to have is that of telling the ordinary consumers of
art which works are good or bad, and why; and
which, therefore, they ought or ought not to look
at, or hear, or read. But, as we have seen, this is the
very thing a critic cannot possibly do, since his evaluations either represent only his own tastes or declare
only the bearing of the work on interests that he has
but that his readers may not share.

The critic's utility, rather, is of two other sorts.
If a person has read often enough of what a given
critic has to say concerning books or pictures or

music with which he is himself familiar, then he may form an idea of the relation between the critic's judgments and his own. He may find, for instance, that he himself usually likes or finds interesting the works that the critic approves; and he may thus be able to infer, from what the critic says about a given book, whether or not he will himself find it worth reading.

The other function of the critic is closely related to this, and may be compared to that of the guide a traveler engages in a foreign city. The guide may save the traveler much time and effort by pointing out sights that he might otherwise have overlooked, or have discovered only with much trouble. Even then, of course, what the guide or the critic can do is only to point out the things, or the aspects of given things, that in his own estimation reward or penalize attention. For once they have been pointed out to the consumer and he has seen them, he alone can decide whether his own estimate of their worth is or is not the same as that of his guide.

What the Philosophy of Art is Good for

This chapter may perhaps best be brought to a close by a brief restatement of the nature and utility of philosophy in general, and in particular of the philosophy of art and of criticism, which, having received a good deal of concrete illustration since its abstract presentation in the first chapter, will now have more definite meaning.

Philosophy, like science, is an attempt to gain knowledge, but of matters different from those that the sciences study. The philosophy of art, accordingly, caters to our intellectual, cognitive, reflective interest; and not—or at least not directly—to the aesthetic, creative, or critical interest that we may also have in concrete works of art. But the intellectual interest—the curiosity—that animates the philosopher of art is curiosity concerning man's aesthetic, creative, and critical interests. And by following the promptings of his curiosity concerning these things, the philosopher is able to obtain on them, and perhaps pass on to others, a perspective that picks out the essence of each of these activities from among the accidents and variations that so easily mask that essence when one is an active participant rather than a curious but impartial spectator.

The value of this—in addition to that which the satisfaction of curiosity itself has for any man who is curious about such things—is that the perspective gained on the whole subject of art, appreciation, and criticism tends to immunize one against infection by the countless dogmas and half-thoughts that infest Bohemia and that otherwise are so likely to be taken either as revelations from on high or as perverse promptings from below.

On the positive side, that same detached perspective is likely to give one a measure of understanding, of tolerance, and even of sympathy, toward tastes that one does not happen to share; toward exploratory or pioneering movements in art that shock many persons, merely because they themselves were brought up on a different sort of art diet; and toward standards of criticism relevant to demands other than those one personally makes on the works of a given art.

Such serenity and catholicity of understanding is one of the chief fruits of philosophy and is, I take it, an essential part of the difference between a merely sophisticated and a truly cultured and liberal outlook.

CHAPTER VI

WHAT ART CAN DO FOR YOU

NOT SO MANY DECADES AGO, the admissibility of the natural sciences to the curriculum of our colleges was a live question. These sciences had to argue their right to share the noble company of the humanities. But nowadays the question often raised is rather whether the study of the humanities is worth retaining, or at least on what grounds. The natural sciences have put into the hands of men unprecedented power to harness to his ends the forces of nature. The telephone, the airplane, the conquest of disease, mass production, and other inventions of our age, which these sciences alone have made possible, are very generally held to show that their study is worth while. But the study of the humanities bears no fruits of comparably obvious sorts. What, then, justifies the pursuit of humanistic studies?

I believe that the case for these studies is even stronger today than in the past, but it cannot be adequately presented unless we are first agreed as to what exactly the humanities shall be held to embrace. The application of that term has grown in rather haphazard fashion. Originally, it included the study of the classics—that is, of the finest literature of ancient Greece and Rome. But today it includes

study of the masterpieces also of other great litera-
tures, and more besides. Grammar, philology, linguistics, and other subjects that, although distinct from
literature, are more or less closely connected with
it are classed among the humanities. Archaeology,
the history of art, and in general the history of civili-
zations would be examples.

It appears, then, that the term "humanities" has
been applied with but little thought as to what it
should imply; and, as its application has become
more and more heterogeneous, its implication has
correspondingly dwindled more and more to nearly
nothing. Our only hope of rescuing the term from its
present vagueness and of finding for it a meaning
both definite and rooted in realities lies in approaching the problem, on the one hand, through a conception of what the education of a complete human
being involves; and, on the other, through an understanding of the specific contributions to it that certain subjects and modes of study alone can make.

When education is mentioned, the idea that most
readily presents itself is perhaps that education consists in acquiring knowledge of a variety of facts and
their relations, and in developing the intellectual
powers required for the acquisition, organization,
and application of this knowledge. But evidently this
constitutes only what may be called intellectual education. For the development of a complete human
being, education of several other sorts is needed in
addition—physical education, to unfold the powers
of his body; religious education, to foster in him

goodness of heart; moral education, to establish in him the habit of dealing justly with all. But there is need also for education of a kind less often explicity mentioned but just as important, namely, pathetic education—that is, education of the feelings. This seeks to open up to man and to sensitize him to ranges and subtleties of feeling for which he has the capacity, but which he would not ordinarily discover unaided.

The term "feelings" is used in the present connection to refer to two large groups of experiences. One of them, to be called for short the sensations, consists both of sensory impressions and of images of imagination. The other group consists of the feelings that may be called the sentiments and includes emotions, moods, attitudes, as well as longings, impulses, dispositions, aspirations, inclinations, and aversions—all of these, however, as felt directly, rather than as intellectually analyzed.

This qualification is important, for language has no names for most impulses or dispositions as immediately experienced, and therefore is compelled to refer to them as impulses or dispositions *to do so and so*. But such a description of an impulse, by riveting our attention on the actions in which it eventuates, easily deludes us into believing that to experience an impulse is to contemplate some course of action; whereas the fact is that every impulse has its own peculiar "feel," which we instantly experience, whether or not we have as yet learned what action it leads to. The impulse to sneeze, for example, has its own characteristic feel, which is experienced even by an infant who, never before having sneezed, does not yet know that the action—sneezing—follows upon the particular feeling he is experiencing at the moment.

The common character of the sensations and the sentiments, and that which accounts for the common name "feelings" being applied to both, is thus their immediacy or intuitiveness—the fact that, however much we may learn *about* them, yet we do not know *them* unless we ourselves have felt their intrinsic quality. Feeling, that is to say, is here contrasted with intellectual knowledge, as in French *"connaître"* is contrasted with *"savoir,"* or in German *"kennen"* with *"wissen."* To express this contrast in English, William James, it will be recalled, proposed the two terms, "knowledge of acquaintance" and "knowledge about."

Education of the feelings, which requires acquaintance with an increasingly wide variety of feelings, brings about development of the capacity to discriminate among feelings—the capacity to discern among them differences, likenesses, and other relations of which we were before unconscious. Discrimination or discernment is commonly described as "the capacity to tell the difference," which is substantially correct. But more accurately it is the capacity, not so much to tell, as to notice a difference; and, indeed, not exclusively a difference, but equally a likeness or other relation to which persons not having had the sort of education now being considered would be blind.

Only a moment's reflection is needed to perceive how essential a part of the education of a complete man and how important, not only to the sensibilities, but often even to the happiness of those with whom he comes in contact is this capacity to distinguish nuances of feeling more subtle and relationships between them less obvious than those that spontaneously thrust themselves upon everyone. As it concerns the sensations, this sensitiveness and capacity for fine discrimination constitutes what is meant by possession of a developed or cultivated aesthetic taste. And as it concerns the sentiments, it alone is what makes possible intuitive apprehension of another's temperament and sympathetic insight into his scheme of values, his motives, his problems, his ideals and aspirations; or, in general, into the emotional meaning or puzzle that life presents from his unique point of view.

This ability to discriminate is thus the indispensable foundation for tactful dealing with others, and for accurate appreciation of the endless variety of human relationships and human situations. Hence, however greatly we may admire a man's moral character and his intellectual attainments, we perceive an unmistakable lack in him if we cannot also say that he is a man of taste and gifted with delicacy of sentiment. A man is not fully human if he is undeveloped in the feeling dimension of his being. The saying that "the road to hell is paved with good intentions" and the remark that "some men of brilliant intellect are yet scoundrels" are but ways of expressing the fact

that piety, righteousness, and intelligence are not
enough. This is brought sharply home to us when
we meet, as we occasionally do, someone who has all
these qualities but who is yet crude of taste, uncouth
of manner, clumsy of speech, tactless, emotionally
immature, or incapable of sympathetic discernment.

How, then, may subtlety and delicacy of sentiment
and a sensitive, discriminating taste be developed?
Man's daily experience in the natural course of his
life normally contributes something to this development, just as it contributes something also to the
growth of his intellectual equipment. But precisely
because the range of development that comes thus
unaided is usually very limited, there is a universally
recognized necessity for deliberately planned education that shall go beyond that range. This leads us
to ask what particular subjects of study and what
particular modes of studying them are especially
adapted to the education of the feelings.

The answer is not hard to discern. Art is the language of feeling; and the works of the various arts
are the expression and record, in communicable
form, of the feelings with which their creators were
inspired. Works of art, that is to say, provide the
means to the desired greater breadth and depth of
acquaintance with the immense variety of human
feelings. Contemplation by an individual of the
things artists have created makes it possible for him
to experience and discriminate many of the end-
lessly numerous feelings with which the unaided
course of his life would certainly have left him un-

acquainted. The products of the various arts, then, are to pathetic education what scientific, historical, or philosophical books are to intellectual education.

But to the distinction made among feelings between the sentiments and the sensations, there corresponds one between the *dramatic* components of a work of art and its *design* components. The word "dramatic" is here used to refer to those aspects of the work that, either through representation of persons and things and of relations that bear on their purposes, or in some more direct manner, express and excite sentiments. The design aspect of a work of art, on the other hand, is impersonal, in the sense that its material is sense qualities themselves; and that the relations used in their arrangement are simply spatial, temporal, or qualitative ones, and not, as in the dramatic aspect of the work, interrelations of human purposes. In some works of art, the design aspect is emphasized, and the dramatic minimized or disregarded; in others, the converse is the case; and in yet others, both are made to play essential parts.

Designs as Materials for Educating the Sensations

Evidently designs, or the design component of works that are not simply designs, will furnish us with the best material for educating our sensuous discrimination and our appreciation of the qualitative and spatio-temporal organization of sensations. We shall gain this education from the study of works of painting, sculpture, architecture, music, poetry;

and of art objects such as tapestries, furniture, fabrics, jades and ivories, lacquers, wood carvings, book bindings, and the like.

But it cannot be too much emphasized that, for the purpose of developing the discrimination that constitutes taste, study must here mean primarily the direct, personal, intimate, repeated, and prolonged contemplation and comparison of diversified examples of objects of the kinds just mentioned. For discursive "knowledge about" such objects has, for the purpose now in view, no importance except insofar as it may prove an aid or a stimulus to contemplation. Although reading, hearing, or talking about works of art may enliven our interest in them and move us to sharper observation of them, nevertheless discourse concerning works of art is never a possible substitute for firsthand observation if our purpose is to develop in ourselves genuine sensuous discrimination and discernment of design form, and not just to stock our memories, for conversational or lecture purposes, with the recorded results of other people's direct observations.

As pointed out earlier, this is something that scholars who teach "art appreciation" need constantly to remember; for scholars are persons whose central interest is in scholarship, and whose inveterate tendency it therefore is to conceptualize whatever their attention touches and turn it into a subject of discourse. In the realm of art, however, this means erecting into an end the pursuit of information that, at best, can be only an aid to the sensitization of taste. It should never be forgotten in this connection that a man blind from birth, but who had studied many books, could give a learned lecture about the history and appreciation of painting, although himself totally incapable even of telling one color from another; and that, on the other hand, even exquisitely sensitive painters have, for the most part, possessed little book knowledge about painting.

Dramatic Literature as Educator of the Sentiments

For the education of the sentiments, as distinguished from the sensations, the appropriate study material will be works of art considered in respect to their dramatic component—dramatic, that is, in the sense already stated of embodying hopes or fears, desires or aversions, or other of the countless varieties and subtleties of human sentiments. Painting, through the representation of persons, human relations and situations, or objects of use, has considerable resources for this purpose. So, too, has music, independently of representation, through its power to express moods and emotions directly, as do the intonations of the human voice. But the art whose dramatic resources probably exceed those of all the others is literature, including thereunder naturally what is specifically called the drama; but also all poetry, the story, the novel, and indeed also biography and much of history, if considered as stories rather than as stocks of factual information.

Such literature makes it possible for the reader

who lives in imagination in the situations it depicts and identifies himself imaginatively with the characters it describes to experience vicariously all the diverse human sentiments that such human beings in such situations and relations would experience. Obviously, there could be no opportunity in the reader's own real life for experience so varied or so costly. And it is worth while to note that, although the situations and roles that literature thus permits the reader to enter or play are entered or played by him, not really, but only in imagination, nevertheless *the psychological insights obtained by him in this way are in no way imaginary, but as genuine and real as any.* A man, for example, may imagine his beloved to be faithless without believing that she is; but when he dwells on this image, the feeling of jealousy, which may hitherto have remained utterly unknown to him, is none the less then genuinely discovered by him and as really, even if not as intensely, experienced as if he believed what he imagines.

The study of literature thus makes it possible for us to broaden immensely our horizon of sympathetic insight into human sentiments and into the human problems or relations to which they relate; but it must be stressed that, for this, the manner of study is again all-important. It must be the manner that alone procures to the student personal experience of the sentiments packed into the literary works he reads. It consists in his entering imaginatively into and living emotionally in the characters, situations,

and relations depicted. On the other hand, study
that consists in reading about such literature or in
technical analysis of it is, for the purpose of education of the sentiments, never a possible substitute for
the reading of the works themselves in the manner
just described. For this purpose, lectures or reading
about a literary work have importance only insofar
as they actually aid us to understand more adequately
the situations into which, through reading the work
itself, we attempt to project ourselves in imagination.

Relevance of Other Studies to Pathetic Education

The rendering of aid of this sort connects to some
extent with the education of the sentiments certain
other studies, generally classed as humanistic, such
as philology, linguistics, archaeology, and the history
of the arts, the philosophies, and the social and political institutions of mankind. To carry on research in
these subjects, however, is something very different
from reading literature in the manner described above
as appropriate to the education of the sentiments. For
research in these subjects is essentially as scientific
a pursuit as is research directed to discovery of the
laws of nature; and the sort of education it specifically provides is, accordingly, not education of the
sentiments but intellectual education—development
of the powers of accurate factual observation, of
scientific explanation and inference, of criticism and
construction of hypotheses.

Yet these studies may be called humanistic sciences,

not only insofar as they provide the reader of literature with the sort of information he needs to understand adequately what he reads, but also and chiefly
because, although their methods are as scientific as
those of the natural sciences, their subject matter consists of the history of human societies; and because
knowledge of their history in its various aspects is
capable, when taken in a certain way, of contributing effectively to the enlargement of our horizon of
attitudes, interests, evaluations, and the like.

How that knowledge is to be taken if it is to do
this is suggested by the observation that when a man
speaks to us, he is always telling us two stories at
once, although commonly we attend to but one of
them. One is the story that the words he utters describe, and it may be about anything. The other is a
story about himself—the story, namely, constituted
by the fact that he, under the circumstances present,
does tell us just that story, and tells it to us in just the
way he does. The style and the matter of a man's
speech or of his writings, it has been said, is a picture
of what the man is—of his point of view, his character, his intellectual resources, his tastes, his temperament. And all this is exhibited to us, if we but
give it our attention, not only when a man expresses
himself in language, but equally where his modes of
expression are of other sorts. How a man walks or
sits, what sort of clothes he wears and how he wears
them, what sort of house he builds, how he spends
his leisure and his money, what he fights for and how

he does it, the undertakings to which he devotes himself, the sort of gods he worships, which books he
reads, the arts he cultivates and the sorts of products
he makes them yield, the modes of conduct and the
social institutions of which he approves or disapproves—all these things provide us with a picture of
the man and of his environment, into which we can
project ourselves in imagination as effectively as we
can into the characters and situations represented in
the stories he tells, the plays he acts, or the books he
writes. And the education we obtain by doing so is of
the same sort in both instances. It consists in enlargement of our insight into the varieties of human
ideals, outlooks, evaluations, and experiences.

To travel abroad, whether in our own country or
another, is universally recognized as something well
worth doing. The value travel has, however, lies
usually, not in what we can do with the outcome in a
practical way, but in what the experience does to us
—in the broadening, humanizing effects it has upon
us, if only we do not insist on taking along intact our
own ways, our own views, and our own associates.
But it does not perhaps occur to many that there is
such a thing as traveling to foreign times as well as to
foreign places, and that this is done by studying and
entering imaginatively into the various aspects of the
history of man as revealed to us by the humanistic
sciences. From such travel in time, the same sort of educational experience is obtained as from travel in space.

Man Practical by Necessity but Imaginative by Inclination

Study in the manner that has now been described of works of literature and of the other arts clearly makes to the education of a human being a sort of contribution that experience in scientific research, whether in natural or other fields, cannot make. But the converse also is true. And it may be insisted that the scientific investigation of the laws of nature and of social phenomena not only educates the intellectual powers but, in addition, yields knowledge of a sort that brings with it power to bend its objects to the service of human ends, whereas neither the study of literature nor the pursuit of the humanistic sciences does this.

Although this is true, yet it is important for a sane perspective to keep clearly in mind two facts. One of them is that, although the applications of natural-scientific knowledge have, whether for better or for worse, transformed human life in the last few generations, only a small fraction of the fruits of the research carried on in fields of natural science has been drawn upon in these applications. The bulk of these fruits has no utilitarian applicability that anyone can now discern, and very likely never will have. Of course, it is to be admitted that apparently quite useless discoveries have, time and again, turned out eventually to have great practical importance; and the chance of this is often held to be enough to

justify all scientific research. But although this is
probably true, to insist upon it is to paint a false picture of the place of research in the life of man. Most
research is, in fact, carried on by those engaged in it,
not because of the applications its results may turn
out to have, but because of its fascination—because
the passion for knowledge is one of the most powerful
motives of man. And this avid interest in knowledge
is not limited to the few who carry on the research.
The public at large, just so far as it is enabled to
understand what the problem is and how it is at-
tacked, is likewise fascinated by it and has the same
disregard of the possibilities of practical application.
The discovery of a new planet, for instance, is front-
page news, as is the discovery of a new Egyptian tomb
or of fossilized dinosaur eggs, although the discerni-
ble "practical" utility of each is nil.

To represent man as being essentially utilitarian,
in the sense that he values and is willing to make
sacrifices only for things that, like electric motors and
other machines, can minister to his bodily needs or
comforts, is thus grossly to distort the facts. The plain
truth is that, by inclination, man is fundamentally
imaginative rather than "practical," and that he pays
to considerations of practical utility as little attention
as he can afford to. It is the ruthlessness of nature
that forces him to give heed to them. And natural
science, which today has reached the point where it is
able to command nature, is hailed as a savior precisely because it is already freeing man from his

dawn-to-dusk slavery to "practical" pursuits, and opening to him a life in which he can give larger parts of his time and energy to the things he really wants to do.

Although the practically applicable fruits of natural science thus constitute the necessary foundation for a life better than that which the mass of mankind has always lived, this foundation is humanly worth having because of the superstructure it can support. Of that superstructure, the pursuit of knowledge for its own sake is an intrinsic part; but so is man's development of faculties other than the scientific, and so is the humanizing of his relations with his fellows.

Great as are the blessings we owe to the natural sciences, it must not be forgotten that these sciences know nothing of good or evil. They place into our hands powers that, compared to those we had hitherto, are as dynamite is to a popgun; but make us no less selfish or greedy, no more honest, truthful, kindly, or wise than before. Thus it is that man turns to them both for poison gas and for anesthetics, both for the torpedoes that sink ships and for the radio that brings help to the survivors. Natural science is not to be blamed for the evil ends to which men, again and again, turn the knowledge it gives them; but if society, now equipped with immense powers, is not to destroy itself through their misuse, the need, today more than ever before, is for the humanization of man.

Some Other Things Art Does for Man

That the works of the various arts are instruments *par excellence* fitted to serve as educators of the feelings will have been made evident by what precedes. But art can do for men a number of other things also, which are no less deserving of attention.

The most obvious of them, perhaps, is to introduce into the environment of man objects whose beauty delights him. Although, as we have seen, an object may be genuinely a work of art without being beautiful, nevertheless the fact is that, as judged by the taste of most men, the majority of works of art have some beauty. This, of course, is true especially of the works of the decorative arts, since in their case there is positive attempt to make the object produced aesthetically pleasing. At all events, works of art which lack beauty in the eyes of those who behold them are neglected and automatically tend soon to disappear unless their failure to give aesthetic pleasure is compensated by merit of some other kind. The craving for beauty is strong and widespread among human beings; and, since it is so no less among those who create works of art than among those who behold them, it naturally tends to function in the artist as does a censor, which determines not so much what he shall do as, negatively, that he shall not do this or that unbeautiful thing unless some positive reason for it compels.

The beauty of beautiful works of art yields aesthetic delight not only when attention is deliberately turned on them, as with paintings in galleries or symphonies in concert halls, but also when they gain only the margin instead of the focus of attention. This is what occurs at times when works of decorative art, such as furniture, silverware, and the like, are being used for the practical functions they were also expected to serve, rather than being attentively contemplated. The same thing occurs also when works of "free" art are being employed, deliberately, as decorative context of some of the activities of ordinary life—for example, when songs are being sung while marching; or, again, when music is being played during dinner; or, as in some factories, while monotonous work is being done.

Works of art, however, function not only as aesthetically pleasing contexts of various activities, but also sometimes, through the feelings they express, as ancillary to certain activities to which these feelings are related. Examples would be the religiously stimulating or inspiring effect of religious music, religious paintings or statues or stained glass, or religious dramas, as contexts of religious exercises in places of worship; or, again, martial music as context of some military exercises.

For the artist—and let it be remembered that most of us do at times engage in creative activity in some art medium, even if at humble levels—art serves not only to relieve the pressure of the emotion which inspires him to create, but also, by objectifying that emotion, his creative activity clarifies it for him and gives him the opportunity to judge it.

A poem one has written, for example, is an objective, scrutinizable record of one's state of soul at the time. On reading it later, one may admire still the sentiments it expresses; or, on the contrary, one may judge them tawdry or naïve or otherwise unfit to own, and one may then repudiate them as being no part of the self one chooses to be henceforth. The creation of things that express the artist's inner state in objective form thus in part serves him as a means of self-knowledge. But it is not to himself only that it reveals what sort of person he is. Others, who contemplate his works and read the feelings expressed in them, learn it also. In this way, art serves to attract to the artist as a person those who find the soul he expresses congenial to their own. But it functions equally to repel from him those who find it uncongenial, and this is no less important. Thus, as pointed out in passing in an earlier chapter, art is an instrument of social assortment, rather than, as H. R. Marshall said, of social consolidation.

It is worth noting, moreover, that the function of art as a means of revealing aspects of one's inner self to others is not confined to the cases where the work they contemplate is of one's own making. The comments two persons exchange concerning the music they both hear, the paintings they both look at, the poems or other works of literature they both read, and so on, likewise reveal each of the two persons to the other, even when the works on which they comment were created by neither of them. Works of art thus are, indirectly but quite effectively, a means of getting acquainted with another person's taste, with the directions of his imaginative interest, and with the nature of his emotional aspirations and aversions.

That art can also serve, for artist or consumer alike, as a form of escape—as temporary vacation from worry, from pain, or from the drab monotony of routine duties—is likewise true. This, however, is not a capacity peculiar to art but rather one it shares with many other activities, and it therefore need not here be more than mentioned.

CHAPTER VII

THE ART OF PERSONAL BEAUTY

M AN, we pointed out earlier, is the animal who is not satisfied with merely living his life, but who is capable of—and insists upon— watching himself doing it. He not only is, acts, feels, and knows; but, unlike any other animal, he is insatiably curious to observe his body, his actions, his feelings, and his thoughts.

When he does this, however, he is seldom wholly satisfied with what he finds. Nature, he discovers, has been both niggardly and clumsy in the appearance it bestowed upon him, and likewise in the talents, virtues, and powers with which it equipped him. Therefore, no sooner does he get a good look at himself than he takes steps to effect, as best he can, changes for the better.

This process of self-editing or self-improvement may, as we emphasized, be directed not only to man's person but also to his personality, in any or all of its various aspects. By the mental activity called reflection, man is able to behold more or less objectively his own manners, modes of speech, conduct, feelings, motives, and thoughts; and when he thus beholds them, he is in position to judge and appraise them, and to do something to mold them to a pattern more to his liking than the one they have at the moment.

Reflection upon what we are and the attempt to transform that into what we should like to be is thus a process closely analogous to that of sitting in front of a mirror and applying to our lips and cheeks the lustrous glow that nature forgot, begrudged, or eventually took away. In both cases, however, the appearance is often much easier to improve than the reality. The kindliness, magnanimity, or patience that we find we lack but would like to possess genuinely does not, alas, come to dwell with us at the mere wish. But the appearance of these qualities is not so hard to put on as the reality. Even when ill will, pettiness, or impatience stirs within us, it is possible, with a little effort, to speak and act the part of good will, nobility, and equanimity.

Shallow criticism will say that to do this is to be a hypocrite and a sham. But although someone has said that "shams are the illegitimate offspring of idealism," we may say with equal justice that the legitimate first-born of idealism makes its appearance at the surface of our personality. For the surface is the easiest part to alter; and, being the place where our contacts with other persons are made, is of much more immediate importance to them than our psychological interior decorations.

Absorption in our inner selves to the neglect of the surface with which others have to deal betrays a degree of self-centeredness verging on what has been called spiritual selfishness. Moreover, it should be noted that a part acted thoroughly and consistently soon becomes no longer a part, but truly oneself. As a man thinks and feels, so indeed does he tend to act and speak; but it is equally true, and perhaps even more useful to remember, that as a man acts and speaks, so likewise does he tend to feel and think. Although, as we shall see, no very sharp line separates the improvement or adornment of our character from that of our person, and in a way both are decorative arts, yet the two are in a measure distinguishable. Evidently, it is with the second that a philosophy of the cosmetic art is primarily concerned.

The sort of picture of ourselves that we attempt to realize when we engage in the embellishment of our person is determined by several factors. One of them, obviously, is the foundation of inalterable fact that nature has wished upon us; for, after all, there are limits to the transformations of our appearance that can be accomplished, even by our best efforts and with the help of beauty doctors, plastic surgeons, and other high priests of the cosmetic art. It would have been hopeless for the late Marie Dressler to attempt to make herself look like Greta Garbo, or for either Laurel or Hardy to try to transform himself into a replica of Rudolph Valentino.

Another factor that determines what we attempt to make ourselves look like is the resources of our imagination. There are persons who have many ideas and others who have practically none, at least in certain directions. The ideas relevant in the present connection are pictorial ideas; and the fact that the pictorial imagination of most persons is limited is the reason why most women do not attempt to design their own clothes, but let fashion designers do it for them. They wisely limit the exercise of their taste to choice from a variety of available designs and to modest attempts to adapt either the fashion to themselves or themselves to the fashion, according as the one or the other seems more feasible.

Lack of pictorial imagination is an equally good reason why most of us really need an expert to design our faces as well as our clothes. But the design of faces is much more haphazard than the design of clothing. The design of men's faces, which is almost entirely a matter of beard and haircut, is traditionally set by the collar advertisements in the streetcars; and any man knows that it is hardly worth while to attempt to dissuade the average barber from denuding completely the sides of his head, even if the top is as barren and naked as the bad lands of Wyoming. If one forbids the use of clippers, the conscientious barber, thinking it is because of nervousness, will sprain a wrist if need be to attain the same results with the scissors—and will expect an extra tip for his trouble! The design of women's faces, on the other hand, is, especially among the young, largely a matter of imitating as far as nature will tolerate the design used by some favorite motion-picture star. Only once in a while do we see a young woman whose head gives any evidence that she has taken objective stock of its basic features, and then intelligently attempted to make the most of them.

The other two factors that determine what we at-

tempt to make ourselves look like are the reactions
we observe in others to certain sorts of human appearance and our own taste. The two are closely connected; indeed, it has even been maintained that our
taste is wholly determined by the approvals and disapprovals of the persons who constitute our environment. For these approvals and disapprovals not only
tend to be imitated by us and used as standards, but
determine also the sorts of appearance that we see
constantly about us. These, by force of habit, we
soon come to consider normal; whereas the sorts of
appearance seen only rarely tend to strike us as queer,
shocking, freakish, or funny.

There can be no doubt that the individual's taste
is in this way influenced considerably by what the
members of his set approve or disapprove. But this
can hardly be the whole story. A person's inborn nature, as well as his subsequent nurture, counts for
something in determining his taste. This is shown, in
the realm of the fine arts and elsewhere, by the fact
that occasionally one man, instead of yielding to the
pressure to fall in step with the taste or ideas of his
contemporaries, succeeds in convincing them or their
successors that not he but they are out of step; so that
eventually they adopt his taste, ideas, or practices.

As regards our person, however, it is doubtless true
that the appearance we attempt to bestow upon it is
determined very largely by the impression we think
it will make on others. The expression of our taste is
thereby instinctively confined within the limits of
what we conceive others will regard as appropriate

and attractive. For the fact need hardly be stressed that our personal happiness and prosperity depend, throughout life, very considerably upon the attitude of the persons with whom we come in contact. Moreover, the contact we have with many of those who can affect our fortunes is often very brief and superficial; and the briefer and more superficial it is, the greater is the importance of the surface we exhibit, since it is then all they have to go by.

To be attractive to others, then, is something of great moment to practically all of us; and, roughly speaking, there are two ways to attract people. One is to be likeable, and the other to be fascinating. The two are not entirely independent, but they are nevertheless distinguishable. Likeableness, on the whole, depends more on realities than on appearances; it is more a matter of disposition and character than of looks, except insofar as the latter may be taken as evidence of the former. Fascination, on the other hand, is a phenomenon much less closely connected with the real worth of its object. It depends very largely upon appearances and upon the effect they have on our imagination. The lover beholds the beloved, not with eyes, but with dreams; and dreams also it is out of which fascination is born in every instance, for fascination is not confined to the experience of people in love. Persons of our own sex, children, animals, and even inanimate things can be fascinating. For some persons cats, for instance, have an intense fascination not possessed by any dog, no matter how well liked; whereas for others the reverse will be the case. For some the ocean, or the desert, or the arctic regions have a similarly quite unreasoned magic.

Fascination, then, has evidently nothing to do with reason and everything to do with imagination. It is the attraction anything has for us when it seems to promise realization of something we half-consciously have been longing to find. And fascination it is, rather than likeableness, that our attempts at self-embellishment serve, even if we are often not clearly aware of the fact. Let us now consider some of the means whereby we seek to make ourselves physically attractive.

Although the phenomenon known as falling in love is only one instance where fascination occurs, it is among the most striking and is doubtless the one that looms largest in the consciousness of mankind. And, although being physically fascinated is by no means all of which the state of being in love consists, it is nevertheless normally a very important—some would even say, indispensable—part of it. It is therefore but natural that physical fascination should be an aim figuring conspicuously in our attempts at self-embellishment.

The most obvious determinant of physical attraction is beauty of person; therefore to become or at least to appear beautiful is the most elementary step in the attempt to make ourselves physically fascinating. Of course, beauty of person is something that is variously conceived by different people; and there is probably no one who has not often been dumbfounded by the outlandish tastes of his or her friends in the matter of beauty in the opposite sex.

But no matter whether we prefer blondes or brunettes, a nose that turns up or one that is straight, a statuesque or a dainty figure, there is nevertheless one thing that practically all of us agree upon as contributing most powerfully to beauty of person. That magically effective ingredient is, of course, youthfulness. And the beauty characteristic of the years of youthful bloom is traceable to such familiar factors as a clear, smooth skin, bright eyes, abundant and glossy hair, sound teeth, rosy color of lips and cheeks, and smooth outlines of limbs and figure, without either obesity or emaciation. It is of such stuff that the beauty of young manhood and womanhood is made, and there is no doubt that upon it very largely depends the greatest physical fascination. Its natural foundation is vigorous health and a good frame; but unfortunately these are not to be had for the asking nor even by hard work, and persons who lack them or who lack the normal appearance of them nevertheless wish and need to be personally fascinating just as much as those who possess such appearances.

Devices That Simulate the Beauty of Youth

This, naturally, is the place where the resources of the cosmetic art are drawn upon. Powders and creams skillfully applied may, to some extent, endow the most unpromising surface with the appearance of the famous "skin you love to touch." Unbelievable things can be done to the eyes, making them seem larger, brighter, and more umbrous than nature ever thought of creating them. Shampoos, dyes, washes, and assiduous brushing can impart to the hair the gloss and color it lacks; and permanent waves, switches, wigs, toupées, and rats help to simulate the luxuriant growth that is not there. Teeth can be bought better looking and more serviceable than those we grow ourselves. The healthy color not brought to our lips and cheeks by swift-coursing red blood comes in a little box. Firmness and elasticity can, in some degree, be restored to the flesh by patronizing a beauty parlor or reducing salon, where we pay somebody to pinch us and slap our faces; and the outlines of our figure can be rounded out by the wearing of judiciously designed upholstery, or rounded in by means of obesity belts, braces, foundation garments, straitjackets, or other instruments of torture.

The sometimes deadly effectiveness of such artifices in simulating the appearances of the beauty of youthfulness is well known to all those who use them, and may further be attested by a law that was passed by the English Parliament in 1774. This law stated that:

All women, of whatever age, rank, profession or degree, whether virgins, maids or widows, that shall from and after this act impose upon, seduce and betray into matrimony any of His Majesty's subjects by the use of scents, paints, cosmetics, washes, artificial teeth, false hair,

Spanish wool (impregnated with carmine and used as a rouge), iron stays, hoops, high-heeled shoes or bolstered hips, shall incur the penalty of the law now in force against witchcraft and like misdemeanors, and that the marriage, upon conviction, shall stand null and void.

The prohibition by law of such devices was, of course, due to the fact that they constituted a form of deceit or fraud—a species of false pretenses by means of which such benefits as reward fascination could be obtained by unscrupulous chiselers, in violation of an unwritten code of fair competition. And this element of fraud or deceit, together with the fact that mere physical fascination is too flimsy a foundation for married life, is doubtless the reason why, until relatively recent years, the use of such cosmetic resources has been considered vulgar or even immoral by persons of refinement. As we all know, however, a decided change in this attitude has taken place in our generation. It would be interesting to inquire into the nature of the transformations in the structure of society that were responsible for this change, but this would take us too far afield. Let us consider rather the possible influence of the advent and growing popularity of certain means of fascination, the philosophy of which is quite different from that of the means just considered.

Self-adornment Distinguished from Self-edital

It should be remarked first that, to be successful, the various means of bestowing upon oneself the appearance of youthful beauty must be used with skill. Thus, as regards cosmetic art at least, Kant's assertion that to be good, art must look like nature, is completely true. For if it is obvious to the beholder that the complexion he sees on a woman's face is her own only in the sense that she paid for it, or that the red of her lips came to them not from the inside but from the outside, then her looks, far from creating in him the impression that she is the possessor of youthful health and beauty, on the contrary shout to him from afar that she does *not* possess these. Thus, unless such devices manage really to deceive, what they do is aggressively to defeat their own purpose— advertising, as they then do, at once our deficiencies, our wish to deceive, and our lack of skill. This is so evident that one is forced to wonder how so many of the persons who use cosmetics can be clumsy enough so to overdo their make-up that its effects have no chance whatever of being mistaken for the reality.

It is when we face this question that we begin to realize that make-up can be an effective instrument of fascination quite otherwise than by attempting to imitate the appearance of young beauty. Let it be noted first that our heads and faces are not the only parts of our persons whose appearance we deliberately alter, for clothing fundamentally transforms the appearance of the body as a whole. And, bearing in mind the distinction between clothing and upholstery, it is evident that the transformation clothing effects is not at all of the nature of make-believe. Although we do occasionally find a man of whom it is

hard to believe that he was not born with a brown
derby or in spats and morning coat, nevertheless we
normally run no risk whatever of mistaking clothing
for the appearance of the human body or of mistaking the beauty clothing may possess for beauty of the
human form. Of course, there are various reasons
why human beings wear clothes: protection from the
weather—for example, sheer stockings in winter;
modesty—exemplified by the constantly diminishing
bathing suits of recent years; and so on. But even
when the function of clothing is to hide the human
form, there is no more possibility of mistaking the
one for the other than there is of mistaking a bush
behind which a man hides for the man himself.

Clothing, then, aside from serving as the mask of
the body that modesty or the climate or the desire for
mystery may require, essentially constitutes *adorn·
ment*. Clothing is fundamentally for us today an ornamental mask for the human form, and whatever
manages to serve as such constitutes clothing. A completely tattooed man, for example, can hardly any
longer be called naked, since a whole picture gallery
always trusts itself betwen his skin and the beholder's
attention.

Now there is no reason why the human head and
face should not be dealt with according to the same
system as the rest of the body—covered, that is to say,
with an ornamental mask. Such a mask—whether tied
on or only painted on—constitutes, not embellishment, as did the deceiving devices already considered,
but adornment. And although adornment, as we now

perceive, is quite different from embellishment, it may nevertheless also be an effective means of fascination. In all probability, many of the instances of make-up that would have to be called unbelievably clumsy if they were intended to simulate the beauty of youthfulness are to be understood as attempts, not at deception, but at ornamentation. When, for instance, a lady stains her fingernails to resemble the claws of a tiger ripping up a sheep, we cannot plausibly suppose that she intends to make anyone believe that the bright crimson color is just the result of vigorous good health; but rather, as in a string of beads, we must assume that it is intended to provide decorative spots of contrasting or harmonizing color.

It is clear, then, that women who proceed in this way are for the most part not as yet wholly conscious of the fact that the alterations they make in the appearance of their hands and faces are no longer based upon the philosophy of traditional make-up. For if they were fully conscious of this, they would make a much fuller use than they do of the resources actually at their disposal. If the reason for staining the fingernails, for instance, is that they may provide decorative spots of bright color, why then confine oneself to stains within the range of reds? That the hitherto unused resources provided by stains of other colors are nevertheless beginning to be realized is indicated by a report in the papers some time ago that a certain woman of prominence actually stained her fingernails green to harmonize with her gown. And if green or blue or golden fingernails, why then not likewise green or blue or golden lips, eyebrows, cheeks, and ears? Especially with colored wigs to match, some wonderful effects could undoubtedly be achieved.

Again, the shape of such a feature as the eyebrow is widely modified today by depilation; and more than one cinema star, we read, shaves off her eyebrows entirely and paints on another pair more beautifully designed. But there is no reason for designing eyebrows in a shape that is even plausible if decoration, rather than simulation of nature, is the aim. Double eyebrows, or forked or serpentine eyebrows might on occasion be more appropriate to the arangement of the hair, or to the lines or fabric of a gown. Indeed, lines or shapes having no likeness to or connection with the features of the human face might well be introduced with most ornamental effect.

A step in this direction, which fashion has at times taken, is that of sticking upon the face a small black patch, sometimes round or diamond-shaped, or in the shape of a butterfly or flower. And of course the people whom we call savages, but whose sense of design is often quite as good as ours and is not hampered by the same set of conventions, do not hesitate to paint upon the face a variety of lines or patterns. It is true that the object here is not so much ornamentation as magical effect, perhaps to ward off evil spirits; but whether these patterns be magical or not, the draughtman's sense of design makes them decorative. On the other hand, many civilized women are well aware that adornment of the human face is a magic that may effectively fascinate good spirits of the opposite sex not yet disembodied.

The Borrowing of Beauty and Other Qualities

Decorative clothing, whether for the body or the face, buttoned on or painted on, is something the beauty of which is easily susceptible of being borrowed by the wearer. The borrowing of beauty, interest, glamor, or other qualities by one thing from another is a very common phenomenon. It depends upon a certain psychological principle, an understanding of which illuminates for us a great many facts that otherwise would be puzzling. It is simply that when a given thing is intimately associated with another, then any noteworthy quality of that other tends to diffuse itself over the given thing and to be regarded as belonging to it.

Jewelers, for example, apply this principle when they give to an inferior or small diamond an ornate mounting. The mounting is intimately associated with the diamond, and the notable beauty that really belongs to the mounting tends to be regarded as inherent in the stone. The stone borrows beauty from the mounting if we do not stop to analyze, and usually we do not analyze so long as we are pleased. A jewel of outstanding beauty, on the other hand, is properly given the least conspicuous mounting possible, in order that the attention may not be distracted from its self-sufficient beauty.

Again, we easily think that the importance, might, intelligence, glamor, lowliness, or evilness of individual men are almost visible qualities; but take away from the man his clothing, his usual setting, and his typical occupations, and those normally almost visible qualities fade from sight. In a Turkish bath, rich man, poor man, beggar man, thief look very much alike.

The fact then that beauty, mystery, interest, grandeur, glamor, or other qualities that fascinate can be borrowed by a person from things possessing them that are closely associated with him is what explains the effectiveness of beautiful, exotic, ingenious, rich, or symbolic clothing as a means of fascination. And it explains also the fascinating effects of adornments other than clothing—such as jewelry, perfume, manners, and mode of speech—especially if we note that this borrowing and lending of qualities closely resembles the borrowing and lending of money. The quality or money that is lent is not always the lender's very own, but often has been borrowed from another lender. This means that, in considering the fascinating qualities that clothing, jewelry, perfume, and the like lend to a person, we can distinguish between the qualities that such adjuncts themselves literally exhibit and the qualities that they only signify and suggest. With this in mind, let us now examine in detail some of these other instruments of fascination.

In the case of clothing, the qualities susceptible of being literally exhibited by it would include beauty of color, fabric, and design; whereas the qualities that clothing may represent and put us in mind of, rather than literally present, would include the rank, wealth, and office of the wearer. The fascination with which a military uniform is said to invest the wearer in the eyes of women is thus due in part to its picturesqueness; but probably fully as much to the romance, bravery, and adventure that it manages to connote. And, analogously, the fascination with which a nurse is endowed in the eyes of men by her uniform largely arises from the neatness, sympathy, dependability, and gentleness it plausibly suggests.

The fascination jewelry may bestow on the wearer is similarly in part a matter of the beauty of its color, fire, or design. But that this is only a part of the source of its effect, and among us the lesser part, is shown by the importance commonly attached to the preciousness of the jewels worn. For, so far as actual, visible beauty is concerned, an inexpensive but indistinguishable imitation is precisely as good as the real thing. If known imitations of precious stones are not esteemed, even when faithful, it is therefore only because, although they look the same, they do not mean the same. They do not connote the wealth, power, position, or high birth that alone permit the possession of truly precious gems. And they do not, therefore, single out the possessor as a person unique among thousands, as do rare stones, paintings, and porcelain, or indeed titles, memberships in exclusive organizations, medals for heroism, championship belts, Ph.D. degrees, or six-inch fingernails.

In the case of perfume also, which lends pleasantness to the user, we find ourselves forced to distinguish
between the pleasantness of the odor itself and the
pleasantness of what the odor calls to mind. The odor
of roast beef, for instance, is a pleasant odor; yet a
woman who perfumed herself with it would hardly
become more fascinating. The same would be true of
the odors of freshly ground coffee, pineapple, fried
onions, or pleasant food odors in general. Such odors,
because of their associations, stimulate us, not to love
and dream, but to bite or swallow. To perfume oneself with them would be to provoke hunger in others
and tempt them to treat us as food—a mode of attraction very different indeed from that which we call
fascination.

It would seem, then, that the only pleasant odors
that can lend fascination to the person who uses
them as perfume are of two sorts. One would include
odors that do not make us think of the object that
produces them—for example, musk, patchouli, am-
bergris, and coumarin. There is no temptation to
view or treat the wearer of these perfumes as we
would the objects from which they are extracted, because most of us do not even know what those objects
are. The other sort of pleasant odors fit to serve as
perfumes are mostly flower odors; for the objects
from which they are extracted, although familiar, are
things of beauty that are themselves able to serve as
ornaments of the person and to lend it fascination.

But beside clothing, jewelry, perfume, or even
manners and modes of speech, there are certain other

more subtle, non-sensuous things from which our person may borrow fascination. I refer to the moral, spiritual, or intellectual traits that together make up our personality as distinguished from our person. Evidently to describe such traits as decorations of the person is to invert what we regard as the normal order of importance, as did the barber who congratulated a customer upon having a large brain, because that meant lots of blood in the head, which in turn made the hair grow. Yet that was the important thing from the barber's point of view, and there is such a point of view. Likewise there is the point of view of the cosmetic art—the art concerned with making our *person* pleasing to contemplate—from which musical talent, a poetic mind, wit, resourcefulness, a courageous heart, a brilliant intellect, and a kind soul are all decorations of the person; for they do serve to adorn it and lend it fascination, notwithstanding that this is not their chief importance.

The word "cosmetic" is derived from the Greek *"cosmos,"* which has been borrowed by modern languages to mean specifically the ordered universe, but which originally means simply order or good order. This derivation of its name would be enough to suggest that the cosmetic art, although often regarded with scant tolerance as but a catering to human vanity, nevertheless has noble connections. As we have seen, it is after all one of the manifestations of the incurable perfectionism that marks off mankind from the animal tribes; since man's ideals are but traits, whether of soul or body, that he would like to see but fails to find when he observes himself. A more philosophical and fairer perspective on the cosmetic art is thus obtained if, in appraising it, we remember that the aspirant who in meditation beholds his soul and strives to improve it, and the worldling who in the mirror beholds his face and likewise strives to improve it, are in truth both engaged in "making up." Both, that is to say, are idealists trying to make up for defects they discover in themselves.